Tipbook
Piano

The Complete Guide

Hugo Pinksterboer

Tipbook
Piano
The Complete Guide

HAL•LEONARD®

The Complete Guide to Your Instrument!

First edition published in 2001 by The Tipbook Company bv,
The Netherlands

Second edition published in 2009 by
Hal Leonard Books
An Imprint of Hal Leonard Corporation
7777 West Bluemound Road
Milwaukee, WI 53213

Trade Book Division Editorial Offices
19 West 21st Street, New York, NY 10010

Printed in the United States

Book design by Gijs Bierenbroodspot

Library of Congress Cataloging-in-Publication Data

Pinksterboer, Hugo.
 Tipbook piano : the complete guide /
Hugo Pinksterboer. — 2nd ed.
    p. cm.
Previous ed.: Netherlands : Tipbook, 2001.
ISBN 978-1-4234-6278-1
1. Piano. I. Title.
ML650.P56 2009
786.2'19—dc22

                          2009010861

www.halleonard.com

Thanks!

For their information, their expertise, their time, and their help we'd like to thank the following musicians, teachers, technicians and other piano experts:

Ted Mulcahey (Moe's Pianos, Portland, OR), Steve Sweetsir (Bucks County Piano, Levittown, PA), Albert Brussee (European Piano Teachers Association/EPTA), Carsten Dürer (*Piano News*), Louis van Dijk, Ronald Brautigam, Michiel Borstlap, Dr. Harm van der Geest, Hans Goddijn (*Pianowereld*), Henk Hupkes (Dutch Piano Technicians Association), Jan de Jong, Jakob Kamminga, Mark Kruiver, Johan Mulder, Floor Nanninga, George Olthof (Estonia), Machiel Spiering, Carin Tielen, Mariëtte Verhoeve-Hehakaya, Arnold Duin (SVGB), Willem and Marie-José de Groot, Luuk Guinee, Bram Groothoff, Corrie de Haan, Arend Hahn, Siem Lassche (Hammond/Suzuki Europe), Hans Leeuwerik, Erik Knecht, Loek Nelissen, Mr. Schinck, Henny Vriese, everyone at Andriessen Pianos, Marcel Riksen, and Gerard van Urk.

About the Author

Journalist and musician **Hugo Pinksterboer**, author and editor of The Tipbook Series has published hundreds of interviews, articles and instrument reviews, and DVD, CD, and book reviews for a variety of international music magazines.

About the Designer

Illustrator, designer, and musician **Gijs Bierenbroodspot** has worked as an art director for a wide variety of magazines and has developed numerous ad campaigns. While searching in vain for information about saxophone mouthpieces, he got the idea for this series of books on music and musical instruments. He is responsible for the layout and illustrations of all of the Tipbooks.

Acknowledgments

Cover photo: René Vervloet
Editors: Robert L. Doerschuk and Meg Clark
Proofreaders: Nancy Bishop and René de Graaff

Anything missing?

Any omissions? Any areas that could be improved? Please go to www.tipbook.com to contact us. Thanks!

Contents

Introduction

Are you thinking about buying or renting a piano, or do you want to learn more about the instrument you're currently playing? Then this book will tell you everything you need to know. It introduces you to the basics of this fascinating instrument before covering more in-depth information on types of strings, the action, pedals, and other elements. It provides numerous tips on auditioning pianos, as well as on maintenance, tuning, and regulation, and it gives you an overview of the history and the family of the piano, and much, much more.

The knowledge provided in this book allows you to make an informed decision when buying or renting a new or a pre-owned piano, and it gives you a well-founded idea of the instrument you're playing — which may definitely help you musically as well. As all popular piano-related jargon is clearly explained, *Tipbook Piano* also makes other literature on the subject more accessible, from books to piano magazines and online publications (see pages 170–173) for more information.

The first four
The first four chapters of this book have been written for aspiring piano players and potential buyers. They introduce you to the endless possibilities of the instrument, explain the very basics of the piano mechanism, and tell you about learning to play, and renting or buying an instrument.

Advanced players

All other chapters are geared towards pianists at all levels, and in all styles of music. Chapter 5 is one of the core chapters of the book. Step by step, you will learn about all of the elements that determine the quality, the playability, and the character of a piano, from the instrument's height or length, to the soundboard, the strings, the hammers and the dampers, the action, and the pedals.

Focus

Understanding what the instrument is about makes it easier to focus on its playability and its sound, two major factors when it comes to finding the instrument you're looking for. Helpful tips that make it easier to judge the instrument's timbre can be found in Chapter 6. The next chapter offers additional information on hybrid or silent pianos and digital instruments, followed by a chapter on the main piano accessories.

US dollars

Please note that all price indications listed in this book are based on estimated street prices in US dollars.

Maintenance, tuning and more

Everything you need to know on piano maintenance is in chapters 9 and 10. Essential background information on the history, the family, the production, and piano brands is covered in the final four chapters.

Glossary

The glossary at the end of the book briefly explains most of the terms you'll come across as a keyboard player. Also included are a complete index of terms, and a couple of pages for essential notes on your piano.

Chord charts

As an essential extra, this Tipbook offers a comprehensive section on chords — so you can start playing right away. Enjoy!

— **Hugo Pinksterboer**

See and Hear What You Read With Tipcodes

www.tipbook.com

In addition to the many illustrations on the following pages, Tipbooks offer you a new way to see — and even hear — what you are reading about. The Tipcodes that you will come across throughout this book provide instant access to short videos, sound files, and other additional information at www. tipbook.com.

Here's how it works. Below the paragraph on practice pedals on page 8 is a section marked **Tipcode PIANO-003**. Type in that code on the Tipcode page at www.tipbook.com and you will see a short video demonstrating how a practice pedal works and what it does to the sound of the instrument. Similar videos are available on a variety of subjects; other Tipcodes will link directly to a sound file.

Tipcode Piano-003
This Tipcode demonstrates the effect of a practice pedal.

Repeat

If you miss something the first time, you can of course replay the Tipcode. And if it all happens too fast, use the pause button beneath the movie window.

Tipcodes listed

For your convenience, the Tipcodes presented in this book are listed on page 136. The piano Tipcodes include demonstrations of how the action works, what various types of pedals do, the range of the piano, and more, adding an extra dimension to this book.

Plug-ins

If the software you need to view the videos is not yet installed on your computer, you'll automatically be told which software you

First, make your selection: Tipcode, chords and fingering charts, or the glossary.

The Tipcode window displays movies, photo series, fingering charts, chords, and explanations of the words used in this book.

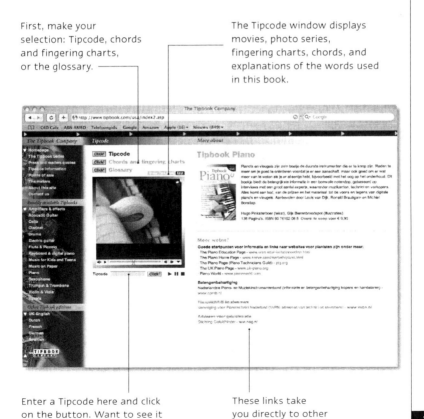

Enter a Tipcode here and click on the button. Want to see it again? Click again.

These links take you directly to other interesting sites.

XIII

need, and where you can download it. This type of software is free.
Questions? Check out 'About this site' at www.tipbook.com.

Still more at www.tipbook.com

You can find even more information at www.tipbook.com.
For instance, you can look up words in the glossaries of all
the Tipbooks published to date. There are chord diagrams
for guitarists and pianists; fingering charts for saxophonists,
clarinetists, and flutists; and rudiments for drummers. Also
included are links to most of the websites mentioned in the Want
to Know More? section of each Tipbook.

Tipbook
Piano

The Complete Guide

1

A Pianist?

Playing solo in a concert hall, at home, or in a jazz club.
Accompanying a choir, a flutist, a ballet company or
a musical. Playing folk music, children's songs, or pop
songs. Music of today or from three hundred years ago.
As a pianist, you can do it all.

As a pianist you can play an endless variety of musical styles, ranging from centuries-old classical music to contemporary hits, and everything in between. More music has been written for the piano than for most other instruments. This is not only because the piano has been around for so long, but also because it is a complete orchestra on its own.

TIPCODE

Tipcode PIANO-001
The piano is a great instrument for all styles of music, as briefly demonstrated in this Tipcode.

Lower and higher

On a piano you can play lower notes than a double bass, and higher notes than a piccolo, the very smallest flute. You can go from note to note really smoothly, almost like a violin, or really hit the keys, making it feel like a drum set. You can play note by note, or play ten or twenty keys at once; both subtle melodies and thundering chords.

Accompaniment

A piano also resembles an orchestra because you can simultaneously play the melody and the accompaniment, and then you can sing along too, as many pianists do. Or you can get someone else to sing, or to play the saxophone, the clarinet, or one of the many other instruments you can play duets with.

Written on the piano

Because a piano is a complete orchestra, a lot of music is written 'on the piano' by classical composers, pop musicians, jazz pianists, cabaret artists, and numerous other musicians. The instrument is a perfect composer's tool.

Playing by ear

On a piano, all the notes are easy to find. They're lined up side by side, from low to high. And there's a separate key for each note. That's why the piano is one of the easiest instruments to use if you want to play a tune by ear. If you need a higher sounding note, you pick a key to the right. And if you want to hear a lower pitch, simply move to the left. Only singing is easier.

Four hundred pounds plus

A piano is one of the biggest musical instruments you can buy: Even a small upright is nearly five feet wide, easily over three feet high, and weighing four hundred pounds (200 kilo) or more. There's one big advantage to that: You'll never have to take your instrument with you when you go out to a performance or a rehearsal. In turn, this means that you have to play the instrument that's available — which may be an enticing grand piano that you

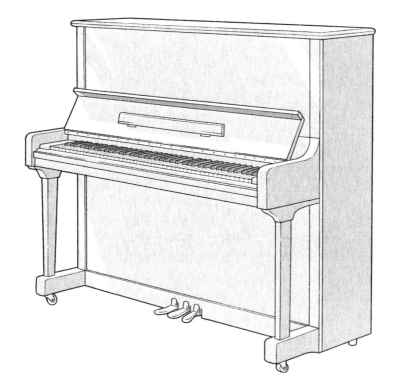

An upright piano...

3

could never afford, an antique, out-of-tune upright with dicey keys, or anything in-between.

> ## Your own instrument
>
> *Many non-classical pianists bringing their own digital piano (see pages 107–109) to a performance, so they're not forced to play the house instrument. Only very, very few classical pianists (and the occasional non-classical musician) travel with their own grand piano!*

... and a grand.

Grand

At most important concerts, whether classical, jazz, or any other style, the pianist plays a grand piano. Being an 'horizontal piano,' even the smallest grand takes up more floor space than an upright or *vertical* piano — and they're more expensive too.

4

2

A Quick Tour

From the outside, a piano looks like nothing more than a big cabinet with a whole lot of keys, a few pedals, and a lid. But all told, a piano consists of some ten thousand parts, most of them inside the instrument. A chapter about a piano's main components and what they do, and about the differences between upright pianos and grands.

Most pianos have eighty-eight keys. If you take a closer look at the *keyboard*, you'll see the keys are divided into alternate groups of two and three black keys. This grouping makes it easy to find the notes you want to play.

... alternate groups of two and three black keys.

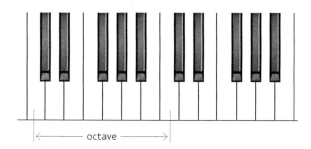

←——— octave ———→

The C and the F

Two examples?

- The white key just before **two** black keys always produces the note C.

- The white key just before a group of **three** black keys always produces an F.

Tipcode PIANO-002
This Tipcode shows where you can find the C and F keys, and demonstrates an octave from C to C.

6

Octave

There are always eight white keys from one C to the next. Such a group of eight is called an *octave*. Within each octave you will find five black keys.

upper panel   lid   music desk   fallboard   keyboard   keybed

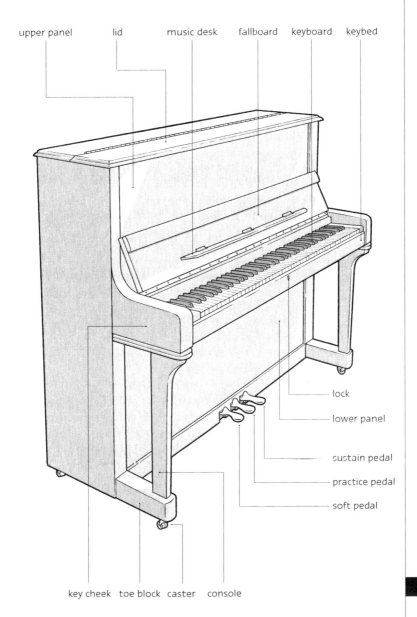

lock

lower panel

sustain pedal

practice pedal

soft pedal

key cheek   toe block   caster   console

Seven octaves

Most pianos have 88 keys. This adds up to a little more than seven octaves. With these 88 keys you can player lower notes than a bass guitar, and higher notes than a piccolo, the very smallest flute.

Hammers and strings

Each key operates a *hammer*, inside the piano. When you press a key, the corresponding hammer strikes one or more strings. The harder you play, the harder it strikes, and the louder the sound. If you let the key go, the sound stops immediately.

Sustain

Most pianos have three pedals. If you press down the one on the right, the sound is sustained after releasing the keys. This explains one if its names: *sustaining pedal*. It's also known as *damper pedal* (see pages 78–79).

Soft

On an upright, the left pedal is the *soft pedal*: It makes the instrument sound a little quieter.

Practice pedal

Pressing the middle pedal on many uprights moves a strip of felt between the strings and the hammers, which muffles the sound considerably. This *muffler pedal* or *practice pedal* allows you to practice without being heard in every room of the house, or in the house next door. Some instruments have a lever instead of this pedal.

TIPCODE

Tipcode PIANO-003
This Tipcode demonstrates the effect of a practice pedal.

8

UPRIGHTS: THE CABINET

Most upright pianos are between 40" and 52" (100–130 cm) high. The width and the depth are pretty much the same for all instruments.

Music desk
On most uprights the *music desk* or *music shelf* is on the inside of the *fallboard*. On others it is mounted on the *upper panel* or *music panel*.

Keybed, legs, and casters
On taller pianos, the *keybed* often has two legs. These legs are purely ornamental. Most uprights with legs have wheels or *casters*, two at the back and two under the *toe blocks*.

Lid or top
When the *lid* or *top* is open, the sound becomes a little louder, brighter, and more direct.

THE BACK

At the back of an upright you will usually find a framework of several chunky wooden posts. These *back posts* support the instrument.

Soundboard
Behind the back posts is a large wooden board, the *soundboard*. When the hammers make the strings vibrate, the strings in turn make the soundboard vibrate. The soundboard sets the air in motion — and that's what you hear.

Ribs
The soundboard is reinforced by the ribs that run diagonally over it. The ribs are also important for the sound of the instrument.

9

Grip handles

The grip handles make it a little easier to move a piano. Only a little, indeed: Even a small upright easily weighs four hundred pounds.

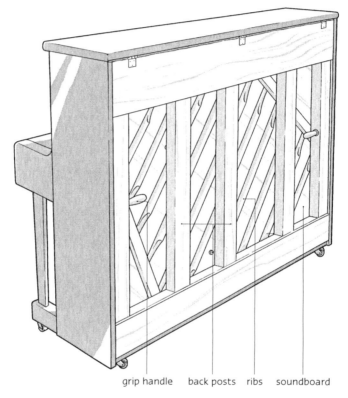

grip handle   back posts   ribs   soundboard

INSIDE

Most piano parts can be found on the inside of the instrument. If you would include every spring, pin, and piece of felt, you'd count some ten thousand items.

Action

Most of these parts belong to the *action*. This is the mechanism that makes the hammers strike the strings. It looks really complicated, but the basics are easily understood.

Jack

When you press down a key, the other end of that key goes up. This sets a number of parts in motion, including the *jack*, which makes the hammer hit the string.

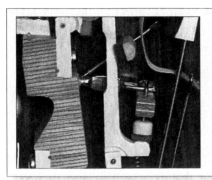

Tipcode PIANO-004
This Tipcode demonstrates the workings of a piano action in slow motion.

TIPCODE

Dampers

As the hammers move towards the strings, the strings' *dampers* move away. The moment you let go of the keys, the dampers return to the strings and the sound stops. That's all, basically.

Ready for the next note

The hammers strike the strings only very briefly. If they would touch the strings for more than a split second, the strings wouldn't be able to vibrate. To enable the hammers to bounce off of the strings right away, the jacks spring back immediately after they have set the hammers in motion. When you let go of the keys, the jacks return to their places, ready for the next notes.

Long and thick, or short and thin

To produce the lowest notes, a piano has long, heavy-gauge strings. A copper winding makes them even heavier. To allow for maximum string length, these bass strings are stretched across the cabinet diagonally. The strings for the highest notes are short and thin.

Three strings per key

Long, heavy strings sound fuller and louder, and they have a longer sustain than short, light-gauge strings. To prevent the low

Four important parts in motion: the key, the jack, the hammer, and the damper.

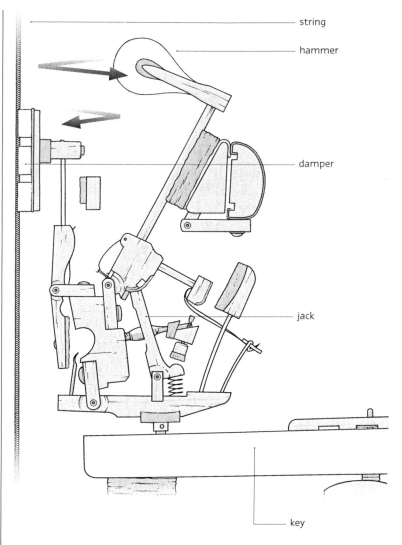

string

hammer

damper

jack

key

notes from sounding much fuller and louder than the high ones, the five highest octaves have three strings per key.

Unisons

These sets of two or three strings per piano key are known as unisons: these strings sound ('son') the same ('uni') pitch.

One or two

In the lowest bass section, each hammer strikes only one string at a time. In-between this section and the highest five octaves are a small number of notes that have two strings per key.

One hammer, one note; three strings tuned to the same pitch.

Twenty cars

In total, a piano has around two hundred and twenty strings. Together, they exert a force of between thirty and forty thousand pounds (i.e., up to 20,000 kilos), the weight of about twenty compact cars!

Frame

To withstand this tension, pianos have a heavy, cast-iron frame. Together with the back posts, this frame or *plate* is the backbone of the piano.

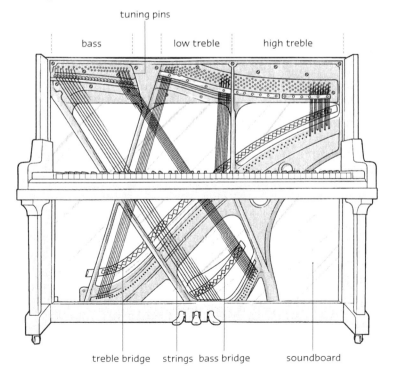

tuning pins

bass   low treble   high treble

treble bridge strings bass bridge   soundboard

13

Tuning pins

The strings are tuned by turning the *tuning pins*, which are set into the *pinblock*. This sturdy piece of work, made up of several layers of wood, is usually hidden behind the frame.

Bass and treble

The strings are divided into three groups. From the top left the *bass strings* run diagonally downwards. The next group of strings is the *low treble* or *tenor*, and the highest octaves are called the *high treble*.

Bridges

All strings run over a *bridge*. This is a long, narrow piece of wood that transmits the vibrations of the strings to the soundboard. The bass strings have their own, fairly short bridge. In the illustration on the previous page some of the strings have been left out so you can clearly see both bridges.

GRAND PIANOS

Grand pianos are grand, indeed. Even the smallest model takes up a lot more floor space than the largest upright. The very longest grands are more than nine feet long and weigh well over a thousand pounds (some 500 kilos). The smallest models are half that length.

Main lid and front lid

The lid of a grand piano consists of two parts: the *main lid* and the *front lid*. When you open the front lid, the music desk appears.

Strings and frame

When the lid is up, the strings and the frame can be clearly seen, as can the soundboard beneath them. Grand pianos have the same number of strings as upright pianos, the bass strings always running crosswise above the other strings. Both uprights and grands are *cross-strung* or *over-strung* instruments.

> ### Lid open
> *If you really want to appreciate the sound of a grand piano, you have to play it with the lid open. At performances, the grand piano is usually positioned so that the open lid reflects the sound toward the audience.*

TIP

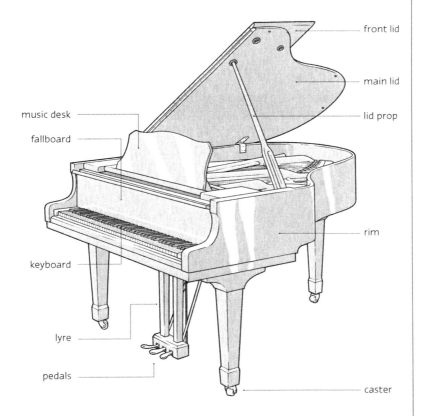

front lid

main lid

music desk

lid prop

fallboard

rim

keyboard

lyre

pedals

caster

Action

An important difference between uprights and grands is that the hammers of a grand piano strike upwards, rather than forwards. That makes everything a little simpler in a grand, because gravity does its bit: When you let go of the keys, the hammers fall back into place by themselves. Likewise, the dampers will drop on the strings.

15

TIPCODE

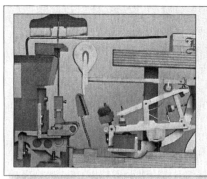

Tipcode PIANO-005
In a grand piano, gravity makes hammers and dampers return to their original position.

More control

This helps explain why the action of a grand piano tends to give you more control over the sound. On a grand, it's easier to go from very soft to very loud, for example, and you can repeat notes at a higher speed. The fact that most grands have longer keys also helps.

Pedals

Most modern grand pianos have three pedals, which are attached to the *lyre*. The sustain pedal, on the right, is similar to that of an upright piano.

Una-corda pedal

The pedal on the left works differently. If you use this *una-corda pedal*, all the keys shift slightly sideways, and so do the action and the hammers. As a result, the hammers strike one less string in each two- or three-string unison.

TIPCODE

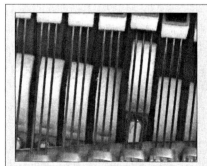

Tipcode PIANO-006
This Tipcode clearly demonstrates that pressing the una-corda pedal makes the hammers hit one string less.

16

Sostenuto pedal

The middle pedal is the *sostenuto pedal*. If you play one or more keys and then press this pedal, those notes will sustain when releasing the keys. All other keys will function as normal, the strings being muffled as soon as you let go of the keys.

Tipcode PIANO-007
In this Tipcode, you can see and hear the effect of a sostenuto pedal.

TIPCODE

THE OCTAVES

A piano keyboard encompasses a little more than seven octaves. To avoid confusion, they have been numbered.

Middle C

The most important key to remember is the C in the middle of the keyboard. This is called *Middle C*, also known as C4: It is the fourth C on the keyboard, counting from the left.

The A

The A to which most instruments are tuned is A4, six white keys or *naturals* to the right of C4.

C40

There are other ways to indicate the various octaves. Some count all the keys, making Middle C C40: It's the 40th key of the keyboard. In European literature, Middle C is often indicated as c'.

17

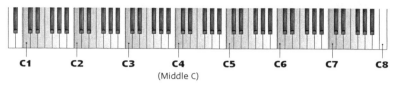

C1   C2   C3   C4   C5   C6   C7   C8
(Middle C)

Other instruments

To give you an impression of how big the piano's range really is, here's how the ranges of some other instruments compare to it.

TIPCODE

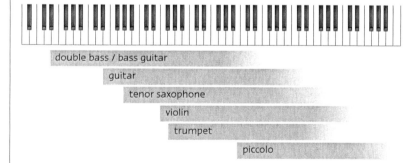

Middle C (C4)

Tipcode PIANO-008
This Tipcodes demonstrates the impressive range of the piano.

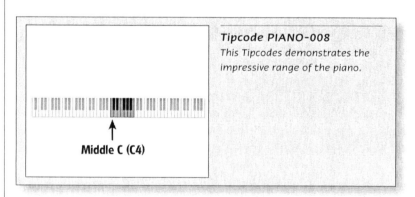

double bass / bass guitar

guitar

tenor saxophone

violin

trumpet

piccolo

3

Learning to Play

Is learning to play the piano difficult? No, because the keyboard makes the instrument easily accessible, and you don't need to learn to play the instrument in tune, like a violin or a clarinet. Or yes, because you are, in a way, playing two parts at the same time: one with your left hand, one with your right. A chapter about just how hard or easy it is, and about teachers, lessons, and practicing.

If you've heard a tune somewhere, it's often easier to play it by ear on a piano than on any other instrument. Why? Because one finger is enough on a piano, and because all the notes are easy to find: higher notes to the right, lower ones to the left.

All ten fingers

To really play the piano you need all your fingers, of course. You usually play the melody with your right hand, in the higher range of the keyboard, and the accompaniment with your left. Or you play two 'voices,' one with the left hand and one with the right, or really wide chords, with four or five notes per hand.

Duets

In a way, even when you're alone you are playing a 'duet' on the piano, your left hand being one musician, your right hand the other. This is one of the things that makes the piano a one piece orchestra.

The upper staff shows the music for the right hand; the lower staff the music for the left hand.

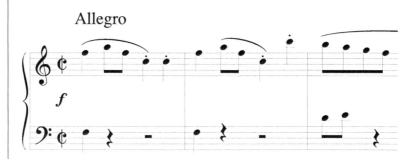

Sonatine, M. Clementi, Opus 36, No. 1 (fragment)

> ### Always in tune
> *One of the great things about a piano is that, if the instrument is properly tuned, you'll never sound out of tune: You don't have to play the notes in tune, as you do on a violin, a clarinet, a sax, or a trumpet. Even so, the better the pianist, the better a piano will sound — believe it or not.*

LESSONS

Of course there are pianists who never met a piano teacher, but by far the majority started off with lessons, whether they want to play classical music or something very different.

Finding a teacher

Looking for a private teacher? Larger music stores may have piano teachers on staff, or they can refer you to one, and some players have found great teachers in musicians they have seen in performance. You can also find piano teachers online (see page 172). Alternatively, you may consult your local Musicians' Union, the band director at a high school in your vicinity, or check the classified ads in newspapers or music magazines. Professional private teachers will usually charge between forty and seventy-five dollars per hour. Some make house calls, for which you'll pay extra.

Collectives

You also may want to check whether there are any teachers' collectives or music schools in your vicinity. They may offer extras such as ensemble playing, master classes, and clinics, in a wide variety of styles and at various levels.

Questions, questions

On your first visit to a teacher, don't simply ask how much it costs. Here are some other questions.

- Is an **introductory lesson** included? This is a good way to find out how well you get on with the teacher, and, for that matter, with the instrument.

- Is the teacher still interested in taking you on as a student if you are doing it just **for the fun of it**, or are you expected to practice at least three hours a day?

- Do you have to make a large investment in method books right away, or is **course material provided**?

- Can you **record your lessons**, so that you can listen at home to how you sound, and once more to what's been said?

21

- Are you allowed to fully concentrate on **the style of music you want to play**, or will you be required to learn other styles, or will you be stimulated to do so?

- Do you have to **practice scales** for two years, or will you be pushed onto a stage as soon as possible?

READING MUSIC

If you have lessons, you'll learn to read music too. It's not really that hard; *Tipbook Music on Paper – Basic Theory* teaches you the basics in a handful of chapters.

Can't read

Of course there are good pianists who can't read music; they're often the ones who can play a piece of music after hearing it just once. Also, there have been countless pieces 'written' on the piano by musicians who couldn't read a note.

Why read?

If you want to play classical music, though, you need to be able

TIP

Klavarskribo

The best known alternative for traditional music notation is Klavarskribo, developed by Dutchman Cornelis Pot. Klavarskribo or Klavar was developed to make reading music easier. It uses black notes for the black keys, and white (i.e., open) notes for the white keys. Notes with their stem to the right should be played with the right hand and vice versa. Other than that, all notes have the same shape: They simply last until the next note appears, unless a stop sign tells you otherwise. The vertical stave has twelve positions: one for each note in the octave. This eliminates the need for sharps and flats. Rests are not required either. Pot introduced Klavar in 1931.

to read music — an ability that has a lot of advantages for non-classical players too.

- If you can read, you'll have access to **thousands of music books**, which allows you to play new songs right away, without having heard them.

- It makes you **more of a musician**, rather than just a pianist.

- And if you can read music, you can **write music** too, from your own exercises to entire compositions.

PRACTICING

You can play piano without reading music, and without a teacher, but there's no substitute for practice.

Half an hour
How long you need to practice depends mainly on your talent and what you want to achieve. Many great musicians have spent years practicing four to eight hours a day, or even more. The more you practice, the faster you'll learn. Most amateur players can make noticeable progress when practicing for half an hour a day.

Three times ten
If playing half an hour at a stretch seems too long, try dividing it up into two quarter-hour sessions, or three of ten minutes each.

TIP

Setting goals
Rather than focusing on how long you need to practice, it may be wise to set a goal for each practice session, or for the next week. This allows you to focus on the music, rather than on the clock — and it can make you want to play more and more each time.

23

Record your practice sessions

No matter how good you are, it's always hard to judge your own playing as you play. *Tip:* Record your practice sessions, or your first or subsequent attempts to play the piece that you have been practicing, and then judge your performance by listening to the recording, once or a couple of times. This is very instructive for musicians at any level. All you need is a portable recording device with a built-in microphone. A computer is great for home recording too!

Plenty of volume

A piano produces more sound than most other instruments. One of the major problems is that a lot of the piano's sound travels through walls and floors to your neighbors and the other rooms in the house. How do you keep everyone happy?

Muffle

Many upright pianos have a practice pedal or a handle that activates a muffling system. This makes the instrument sound much softer, but it also makes the keys feel less direct (see page 80). These systems can be retrofitted.

TIPCODE

Tipcode PIANO-003
A built-in muffler, activated by the piano's practice pedal, strongly reduces the volume of the instrument.

Agree when to play

It's always worth talking to your neighbors and housemates to agree set practice times. This often works well and costs nothing.

Walls and floors

You can take steps to reduce the amount of sound traveling

24

through walls and floors. On hard floors it can help to put the instrument on special *caster cups* (see pages 115–116) or other sound-absorbing material. There is little point in placing muffling materials between the piano and the wall, as this mainly makes the instrument sound dull while hardly reducing the loudness. Insulating the entire room is another option, be it an expensive one. First, read one of the books available on the subject, or consult a specialized contractor.

Silent pianos

Any piano can be provided with a system that allows you to play the instrument using headphones, so no one hears you play at all. These *silent systems* include a rail that stops the hammers right before they hit the strings. The sound you hear through your headphones comes from a *sound module*, mounted under the keybed. The system turns your instrument into a *hybrid piano*: It's both an acoustical and a digital instrument. They're also referred to as *silent pianos*. There's more on these instruments in Chapter 7.

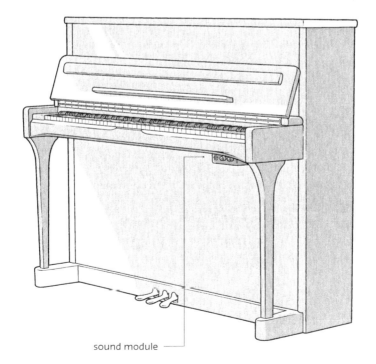

A piano with a basic sound module.

sound module

Digital pianos

Rather than buy or retrofit a piano with such a system, you can get yourself a digital piano. A digital piano has no strings. Instead, it uses *samples* (digital recordings), just like a sound module. Though the good ones sound real close to regular 'acoustic' instruments, they're still different. One major point is that the sound comes from speakers or through your headphones, rather than from a wooden soundboard. The action is slightly different too.

TIP

> ## More information
>
> *If you want to know more about digital pianos, please refer to Chapter 7, and also check out Tipbook Keyboard And Digital Piano. If your budget allows for it and you have enough room, you may also consider buying a digital piano in addition to an acoustic instrument. This may cost less that what you'd pay extra for a silent piano, but the latter has two major advantages: It takes up less room, and the difference in the using the instrument acoustically or digitally will always be smaller then the difference between playing an acoustic piano or a digital instrument.*

CDS, COMPUTERS, AND MORE

Next to the many piano books available, you can use all kinds of different media for practicing too. For instance, there are CDs on which the piano part has been left out. So you can play with a full orchestra, or with another pianist, or play a duet with a violinist, without actually having to get real musicians to join you.

Computerized lessons

As you can read in Chapter 7, digital pianos and the sound modules of silent pianos can be hooked up to a computer, which can be turned into a private teacher by using the required software. You can also use your computer for practice without hooking it up to your piano. For instance, there are programs that can slow down difficult phrases without changing the pitch, so you can find out how they were played note by note. Other programs teach you how to read, or simulate a complete band or orchestra for you to play along with — and there's much more.

Video lessons
There are video lessons too, most of them aimed at styles other than classical music, be it jazz, blues, rock, or some other style.

Metronome
As a pianist you have to be able to keep time, just like every other musician. That's why its good to practice with a metronome now and again. This is a device that beeps or ticks, so you can tell right away when you're speeding up or slowing down. Sound modules and digital pianos typically have a metronome built in.

Listen and play
Finally, try to attend as many concerts as you can. One of the best ways to learn to play is seeing other musicians at work. Living legends or local amateurs – every concert's a learning experience. And the best way to learn to play? Play a lot!

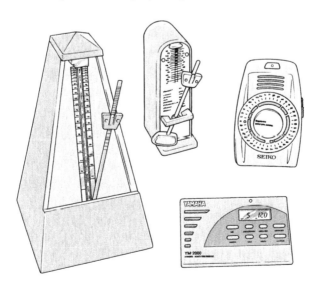

Two mechanical (clockwork) and two electronic metronomes.

27

4

Buying or Renting?

Even the cheapest new pianos cost some fifteen hundred dollars or more. On the other hand, a good piano will last for decades, and it keeps its value well. If it's still too much money to spend all at once, or if you first want to try an instrument out for a while, you can rent one. A chapter about piano prices, about buying, renting, and leasing, buying new or pre-owned instruments, and about piano stores. In Chapter 5, A Good Piano, you'll learn about what to pay attention to once you're in the store.

Considering the huge cabinet and the thousands of parts of the action, fifteen hundred dollars isn't all that much money for a new upright piano — yet there are instruments with that price tag. The most expensive uprights will set you back some sixty grand!

Grand pianos
Grand pianos cost more indeed. They start around seven or eight thousand dollars; top of the line models may cost thirty (!) times as much.

Long-lasting
Because they last a long time, good pianos have a high trade-in value. If you exchange your instrument for a more expensive one, you may even get back what you originally paid for it, or just a little less.

A decent piano
If you are looking for a new upright piano that isn't too expensive but sounds good, plays well, stays in tune, and will probably last at least ten years without major problems, expect to pay three to four thousand dollars or more. If you want to pay less, you can't set your sights as high.

A richer tone
The difference between expensive and low-budget pianos is not easy to see. What are you actually paying for if you spend more money? In the first place, more money will typically buy you a better sounding instrument.

Taller is bigger
When comparing uprights within one quality range, more money will often buy you a taller instrument. The taller an upright is, the 'bigger' it can sound. Do note, however, that there are great-sounding small uprights, as well as 48" instruments that sound relatively 'small'. Four thousand dollars typically buy you a decent 42" instrument.

Better materials
When building more expensive pianos, there will typically be

more hand work involved, and more expensive materials will be used, such as higher quality wood, which has been dried for years so that it won't shrink or swell anymore; better felts for the hammer heads and the dampers; better strings; a finish that has been applied with more care and in more coats so it looks better and lasts longer. All these and so many other elements help make for an instrument that sounds better and is more enjoyable to play.

Life expectancy

More expensive pianos also tend to last longer — up to some four times or more. Of course, the exact life expectancy of any instrument strongly depends on how often it's played and tuned, on how well it's maintained, and on its surroundings. If air humidity and temperature are fairly constant, a piano will usually last longer (and require less tuning!).

Lesser quality

Is there such as thing as a lesser quality piano? Yes. Think pianos that go out of tune quickly, for instance, or pianos that are made from wood that has not been properly dried and cured, so that keys, panels, and other parts may warp. Unfortunately, it's hard, if not impossible to find out these things in a showroom.

TIP

Upright or grand?

Money and space provided, many pianists prefer a grand piano. After all, the upright was invented only because grands take up so much room. So is a grand always better? Not necessarily, and certainly not if you're talking about instruments of roughly the same price. And it does make sense that an expensive upright will typically be a better instrument than a low-budget grand.

The other one

When in doubt between the two, some prefer the feel, the sound, or possibly the looks of a small, affordable grand, while others go

31

for the upright, because it sounds or plays better, or takes up less space. Always remember that lots of pianists who went out to buy a grand ended up buying an upright — and vice versa.

PRE-OWNED PIANOS

Pre-owned instruments can be bought privately, through classified ads, via family or friends, or from a piano store or a piano tuner. Prices range from next to nothing — usually for pianos that haven't been played or tuned for years — to thousands of dollars. Expect to pay about a thousand dollars or more for an upright that you'll enjoy playing for a number of years without expensive repairs.

Appraisal
If you're buying a pre-owned piano from a private party, have it appraised before you buy, even if it's a really inexpensive instrument: If a four hundred dollar piano really needs a lot of work, it can easily cost a thousand dollars to make it playable. Judging a piano on its technical merits, rather than its sound or its feel, is something that should be left to a piano tuner or technician. A written appraisal usually costs between seventy-five and a hundred and fifty dollars, and this expense may save you a lot of money. The report may also tell you what needs to be done to the instrument, and what it'll cost.

Piano stores
Rather than buy privately, you might look for used instruments in piano stores. This may be a bit more expensive, but it has a lot of advantages.

- First, the instruments will usually be inspected, **tuned**, voiced, and regulated.

- You can choose from a number of instruments, which allows you to **compare** them.

- You can come back if you have **questions** or if problems crop up.

- Also, you can be confident that you're **not paying more** than the instrument is worth.

- The instrument will usually come with a **warranty**. Some warranty certificates even show which parts, if any, have been replaced or reconditioned.

Technical buying tips for used instruments start on page 83.

Old pianos

You may run into a very old piano for a very modest price. Is such an instrument good enough for a beginner? If you're lucky, it is. But if the instrument isn't properly adjusted, if the mechanism staggers, and if it can't be tuned anymore, no beginner will ever get beyond that very first beginning. To make an instrument like that playable again will probably cost more than it's worth — so it's usually better to look out for something less of a bargain.

RENTING A PIANO

Rather than buying a piano, you can rent one. The monthly rental fee is usually set as a percentage of the retail price of the instrument. Expect to pay one to two percent of the instrument's retail price. In other words, a five-thousand-dollar piano may cost you fifty to a hundred dollars per month.

The basics

It is impossible to provide a detailed description of the infinite amount of different plans, terms, and conditions you will likely encounter when you decide to rent an instrument. But here are the basics:

- Many rental plans are actually **rent-to-own plans**: The instrument is yours once the periodic payments you've made equals

33

the list price. Note that this list price will usually be higher than what you would have paid had you just bought the instrument outright. This explains why most of these plans are interest free.

- Most of these rent-to-own or **hire-purchase plans** also have an option to buy the instrument before you're fully paid up; if you choose to buy the instrument, your rent paid to date will usually be applied to the instrument.

- With a **lease plan** — also known as a straight rental plan or rent-to-rent plan — you simply keep paying rent until you return the instrument. Rates are usually lower on these plans than those of rent-to-own plans. With these plans, renting for a long period of time will be, of course, more expensive than buying the instrument.

Minimum rental period
Is there a minimum rental period? You may have to rent a piano for at least six months at one store, while you can rent a piano per month somewhere else.

Maintenance and insurance
Tuning can be included in the rental fee, but it may also be offered as a separate expense. The main thing is to make sure you don't have to worry about it. Insurance may be included as well. Make sure you understand what is and isn't covered under your lease or rental plan.

- Does the fee **include** delivery, a bench, tuning, maintenance, and finance or bank charges?

- If **insurance** is included, what does it cover?

- Do you have to pay an origination fee, an application fee, a deposit, or other fees? These **fees** are usually non-refundable; they often may be applied to the rental, however.

- Note that stores may ask for a **deposit** or require your credit card details.

THE STORE

The more instruments a store has on display, the harder it can be to choose one. That said, the more instruments there are to choose from, the better the chance that you'll find exactly what you're looking for. It's especially important that you are given the time and space to play the instruments, preferably more than once, and that the staff is knowledgeable and enjoying their work. In a good store, you'll often find that they can play the instrument too.

Sound advice
Good information is crucial when it comes to pianos, because it's not easy to spot the differences between them, and because the piano is an expensive instrument that you want to enjoy for years to come. Good information is also important because pianos may only show their true quality after months, or even years.

Discuss
This book offers a good deal of the information that you need to make an informed purchase, but personal advice from a trust-worthy dealer remains essential. A good salesperson will help you make your personal choice by discussing things like the type of music you play, how long you've been playing, your preferred type of sound, the piano you're used to and the room the instrument will be played in, rather than simply telling you which piano you should choose.

TIP

Tuned and ready to play
In a good store, all instruments will be tuned and ready to play. You shouldn't buy a piano that hasn't been tuned, if only because you won't be able to hear its true sound. What about a piano that doesn't play well? The problem may simply be poor regulation. If you are thinking of buying it you should definitely wait until the instrument has been regulated before you choose — and be sure to try it again first.

35

Go back

Most piano dealers won't mind if you come back a few times. Most likely you'll need to, in order to make your best choice. Many buyers will visit a number of different stores over a period of a week or so. Not only to compare the instruments by different makes, but also the stories that go with them. Have you fallen in love with a piano at first sight? That's usually a good sign. Still, it's no bad idea to come back the next day to listen to the instrument once more.

Try it out

Pianos hardly ever sound the same in the store as they will in your house. It's possible, though unlikely, that a piano turns out to be a disappointment once it has been delivered at your home. Some stores allow you to exchange the instrument; others let you try the instrument out at home, or they have try-before-you-buy rental programs for a day, a week, or a month.

The same one

No two pianos sound exactly the same, even if they're identical instruments. So always make sure you get the piano you selected in the store, and not the 'same' one from their warehouse. To be on the safe side, you can ask to have the serial number of the instrument noted on your receipt.

Another piano

Some stores apply the full price you paid for the piano you bought at that store toward the price of a new piano, provided you come to buy one within a certain period of time, say one or two years. Usually, the new piano should have the same or a higher retail price than the first one. Again, ask for the exact conditions before you buy.

Warranty

Carefully study what is and what is not covered by the instrument's warranty. For example, it should cover both parts and labor. After all, it may cost hundreds of dollars to replace a relatively cheap part. A long term warranty (fifteen, twenty years, or even more) sounds attractive, but may not add a lot to your investment: Usually, defects that are covered by the warranty will emerge within the first years. Most companies offer a five to ten-year warranty.

Tips

- Please note that warranties are typically valid only if the instrument is sold by an **official dealer**.

- Check if the warranty is **transferable** to another owner, just in case you should decide to sell the instrument.

- Always read the **warranty agreement** carefully, and compare warranties from store to store and company to company. Good pianos are always backed by a solid factory warranty. Distributors and stores may offer additional warranty.

Financing

Some stores offer financing possibilities. Always compare the conditions with those offered by your bank.

FINAL TIPS

A piano is one of the few instruments that you don't tune yourself. In most cases, the instrument needs to be tuned twice or three times a year. Including the required additional maintenance, this will usually cost some two to three hundred dollars per year.

TIP

> ### Tuning more often
> The more often you have your instrument tuned, the sooner you will discover that it's going out of tune: Your ears get used to a proper tuning. The same may happen if you own a silent piano: If you use the built-in digital instrument from time to time, you can soon tell when the acoustic instrument goes out of tune.

37

Take someone along

When you go looking for an instrument, take along another piano player — especially if you don't yet play yourself, and when you're out to buy a privately owned instrument. Sharing your ideas on how the instrument plays and sounds often makes it easier to come to a well-founded conclusion, and four ears simply hear more than two.

More information

If you want to make an informed purchase, stock up on piano magazines, and on all the brochures and catalogs you can find. Besides containing a wealth of information, the latter are designed to make you want to spend more than you have, or have in mind, so ask for a price list too. The Internet is another good source for up-to-date product and price information, and of course there are many more piano books as well. You can find more about these resources beginning on page 170.

Fairs and conventions

One last tip: If a music trade show or convention is being held in your area, check it out. Besides lots of instruments you can try out and compare, you will also come across plenty of product specialists, as well as numerous fellow pianists who are always a good source of information and inspiration.

5

A Good Piano

Choosing a piano becomes easier if you know more about the instrument. This chapter focuses on all tangible and visible aspects of the instrument, and how they may influence its performance: from the dimensions and the cabinet to the action, the pedals, and the strings. Tips for judging pre-owned instruments are also included. Chapter 6 concentrates on what to listen for when choosing a piano.

Just about all the parts of a piano contribute to the tone of the instrument, from the back posts to the strings, and from the soundboard to the hammers. What makes a piano different from most other instruments is that you can't simply replace any of its parts to influence the tone. Saxophonists can experiment with different mouthpieces and reeds, violinists may improve their tone and performance by trying out various strings and bows, but pianists basically have to make do with the instrument as it is. That makes choosing the right instrument so essential, when it comes to pianos.

Voicing

However, it is possible to have the tone of a piano adjusted or improved, for instance by making the hammers softer or harder (*voicing*), and of course you can have the strings or the hammers replaced — but that's basically only done when they're worn out, and the instrument's condition makes such an investment worthwhile. Mind you, these are all jobs for a professional. There's more on this in Chapter 10.

The sum of the parts

In a piano, the tone is the sum of all the parts. No one instrument is ever better than another just because a better type of wood has been used. What matters more is whether that type of wood suits that particular instrument.

DIMENSIONS

The height of an upright piano is a very important dimension. The very smallest uprights are about three feet high (35"; ca. 90 cm), and the tallest about a foot or more higher (48"–52"; ca. 120–132 cm), although occasionally you may see even taller ones. A taller instrument has a bigger soundboard and longer strings, which together produce a 'bigger,' more resonant sound and more volume. This goes for grand pianos too. In most concert halls you'll find a grand piano around 9' long.

TIP

It's all in the name

Many companies indicate the height of their pianos in the model names they use. In other words, a model KJR110 will probably be 110 centimeters high.

Louder, but just as soft

It's quite easy to hear the difference between a smaller and a taller upright of the same quality. The tall one will typically generate a richer, fuller, more powerful and resonant tone. Also, if you play it louder, it may produce more volume, yet it can sound just as soft as the smaller model. The differences are usually best heard in the lower octaves.

Different feel

A tall piano will also feel different to play than a real small one. The lower the piano, the more the action has to be adapted to fit the reduced dimensions (see page 60).

Size isn't everything

Of course, the quality of an instrument is more important than its height alone. An expensive 48" (120 cm) piano can easily sound 'bigger' and richer than a taller but lower-budget instrument. What if you have to choose between two models of the same price, one a little taller and the other a little smaller? Then just buy the piano that sounds the best and that you feel most comfortable playing. Size isn't everything.

How much more

How much you pay for a few extra inches — and tone — depends, among other things, on the make and the price range. If, for instance, you pay around three thousand dollars for a 43" (110 cm) instrument, one piano maker will charge you a thousand dollars more for a 47"; while another brand lists the taller piano for an extra two grand. Why the difference? Perhaps because the second manufacturer installs a better action in the taller model, and the first one does not.

> ## It's the soundboard that matters
> Some taller instruments simply have an extra tall cabinet. Of course, they don't sound any bigger than a piano with a smaller cabinet but a soundboard that is the same size.

Spinet, console, or full-size
The shortest upright pianos are called *spinets* (up to some 40" or 100 cm high); the tallest models, known as *full-size uprights*, are usually between 48" and 52" (120–135 cm). In-between are *console* and *studio* pianos. For most companies, a 52" is their tallest model. Some make 54" or 55" instruments as well.

No standard sizes
There are no standard sizes for these types. For instance, some say that studio pianos range from 43" to 47", others use the same name for pianos of 49" and upwards. You may also come across different names, like *consolette*, which is a small console.

Space
A tall piano looks much bigger than a small one. Even so, both usually take up the same amount of floor space. Most pianos are between 22" (55 cm) and 24" (60 cm) deep. They're all about the same width too.

Grand or upright?
Does a grand piano always sound 'bigger' than an upright? No. It often seems that way, partially because grands are usually played with the lid open, and uprights with the lid closed. What about the size of the soundboard? The soundboard of a 5.5' grand piano (175 cm) is often about the same size as that of a 50" (130 cm) upright, so you would only expect to hear the difference from grand pianos that are longer than that.

Choosing
Having said that, there are other differences to take into account. An important one is that the sound of a grand piano, with its lid

open, can spread out freely in all directions from the soundboard, which is much less the case with an upright, the soundboard usually being close to the wall. Many pianists feel much more 'inside the sound' when they play a grand piano. And yet pianists sometimes opt for an upright when they were looking for a grand. So, if you have the money and the space for either, it comes down to playing, listening, and comparing.

A 9' (275 cm) concert grand piano and a 5' (150 cm) baby grand.

Grand piano names
The smallest grand pianos are often referred to as *baby grands*. They're usually 4'6" to 5'6" (135–165 cm) long. The longest models, called *concert grands*, typically measure about nine feet (275 cm), and a few companies produce even longer ones. In-between sizes are known as *medium grands* or *small concert grands*.

The difference
In a concert grand, the soundboard is nearly twice as big as in a baby grand, and the longest string is about twice as long. It doesn't take a trained ear to spot those differences.

More feet, more dollars
If you go from a 5'10" foot grand to a similar instrument one foot longer, the latter may easily cost you an additional ten thousand dollars. When it comes to the very best instruments, the price difference is likely to be two or three times as big.

43

THE OUTSIDE

Uprights and grand pianos come in a wide variety of styles and finishes, from high-gloss black to wood finishes in many different colors, and from very basic to very modern designs and impressively-carved rococo models.

High-gloss black

High-gloss instruments are treated with a thick coat of polyester or finished with traditional or polyurethane (synthetic) lacquer. The glossy high-polish polyester coating, as used by most European and Asian makers, is pretty tough. Small scratches can be dealt with quite easily, and the finish shines easily. Traditional lacquer requires more care. Black is the most popular color for high-gloss instruments, followed — at a large distance — by white.

Silk-gloss or satin

The advantage of silk-gloss or satin instruments is that they don't show up dust, fingerprints, and other grime as clearly.

Transparent

The same goes for transparent finishes, high-gloss or satin, that allow you to see the veneer, i.e., the thin ply of wood used on the outside of the instrument. Common types of veneer include oak, mahogany, cherry, and walnut, and often several types are combined. Each type of wood has its own hue and pattern.

Unfilled

On some instruments you can more than just see the wood, you can feel it too: The grain has not been filled.

Wax

There are also matte-finish instruments available in which the wood is protected using wax instead of lacquer.

Synthetic outer ply

Low-budget upright pianos can be finished with a synthetic outer ply rather than wood. This makes the instrument less expensive to make and easier to maintain.

_TIP

> ## French polish
> French-polished *instruments are finished with shellac, a natural (usually black) finish with a warm, silky sheen. Applying it is labor intensive and thus a costly affair, and the finish is rather vulnerable, being very sensitive for moisture and direct sunlight. Nowadays shellac, a common finish until the middle of the previous century, is mostly used to restore precious older instruments.*

Custom designs
Some manufacturers offer pianos in custom colors and designs, the only problem being that you can't play the instrument before you decide to buy it. Some piano stores may finish pianos themselves: You first choose an instrument and then have it finished in your favorite color or design. Other companies offer instruments in various (hand) painted designs, or pianos with sparkling keys and other visual effects.

Inside
The panels are almost always finished on the inside too. This protects the wood and reduces the chances of warping.

More expensive or not
Some companies charge you more for a high-gloss finish; others have higher list prices for satin finish instruments. These differences may depend on the type of wood used to finish the instrument, for example; e.g., cherry costs more than oak. There's almost always an additional charge for special colors and finishes.

Details
Instruments can be made more attractive with walnut strips around the edges, upper panels with inlaid ovals or other decorations, chrome-finish instead of gold-colored (brass) pedals,

45

hinges, and locks, special wood types on the inside of a grand cabinet, and so on.

A Chippendale piano (Seiler)

Modern piano (Sauter).

Rococo grand (Blüthner).

Matching your interior

Many manufacturers also produce instruments that match interiors in a particular style, ranging from 21st century design pianos to Chippendale uprights with artfully twisted legs and other ornate features, or heavily decorated rococo-style grands. Some manufacturers offer a choice of three or more styles for each series of pianos, such as Queen Anne, Country Classic (American Colonial design), and Italian or French Provençal.

Decorations

Apart from the color and the height, pianos may have many other small differences that you'll notice only if you know what to look for. A few examples: The corners of the keybed may be rounded or angular; the edges of the lids may be sawn straight, or they may be curved; the legs may be round, square or double, they may be fluted or not, and they may run straight down or taper toward the bottom.

47

... if you know where to look...

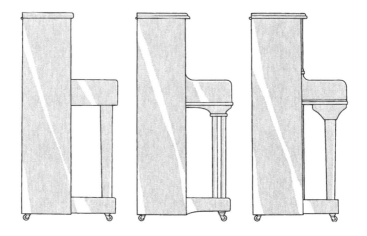

With or without legs

There are three basic styles of cabinetry for uprights: without legs, with free-standing legs, and with legs and toe blocks. The latter type is often a taller piano, referred to as *institutional* or *professional*. Smaller pianos without legs are known as *continental* instruments, the smallest ones often having an upper panel that's slanted backwards. The third type usually features a decorated cabinet and legs, hence the name *decorator style*.

On small continental models, the upper panel is often slanted slightly backwards.

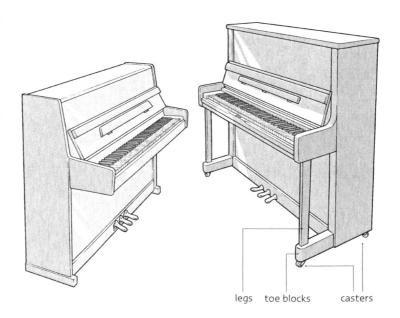

legs   toe blocks   casters

Decorator style piano with free-standing legs.

Casters and wheels

Casters make an upright a little easier to shift around a room, but you shouldn't really use them to move it any distance, especially if the instrument has free-standing legs. If a piano needs to be moved around frequently, you will need bigger wheels. Such

A school piano with locks, brackets and large wheels.

wheels are fitted to *school pianos*, which also have other extras like protective brackets, a lock for the lid, and sometimes a wooden plate to protect the soundboard.

Grand piano casters

Grand piano casters come in various sizes, some featuring a brake. Special sets of wheels that make moving a grand piano even easier are also available.

Grand piano casters in various sizes, with and without a brake.

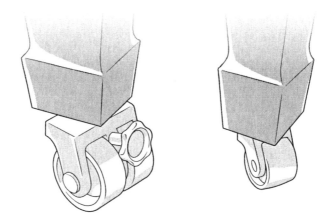

Higher keyboard, higher seat

• Fitting casters or larger wheels to a piano will **raise the keyboard**, which possibly means you may want your seat to be a little higher (see pages 112–113).

• **Changing pianos** may require that you change your seating height too. The white keys sit anywhere from 26" to 28" (66–72 cm) above the ground. Do note that those two inches are quite a big difference.

• If the **keyboard sits too low** for you, the piano can be put on special caster cups (see pages 115–116). Do watch out that the pedals don't end up too high.

Mind your knees

If you have long legs, pay attention to the height of the bottom of the keybed, which usually ranges from about 24" to 28" (60–70 cm).

LIDS, CABINETS, AND BACK POSTS

The large panels and posts of a piano are not the most important components when you are choosing an instrument, but there are a few things that are worth knowing about them.

Fallboard

On most upright pianos, the fallboard or *fall* consists of two hinged parts. That's easier to make than a curved, one-piece fallboard. On some instruments the fallboard is provided with a *soft-fall*, *soft-close*, or *slow-close* system that prevents it from slamming shut (and hurting the players' fingers).

TIP

Pads

To prevent damaging the finish, uprights may have two small rubber pads that catch the fallboard when you open it. Just to be on the safe side, always check that the fallboard easily opens and closes without rubbing at the sides.

Locking the fallboard

If the fallboard doesn't have a built-in lock, you can buy a U-shaped lock that fits around it. There are also built-in and retrofittable locks that lock the fallboard from the side.

Music desk

On most uprights the music desk is usually 24"–34" wide (60–80 cm). The wider models can hold four sheets side by side. To stop the music from sliding off, music desks often have ridges or a raised edge, or they are lined with felt, leather or vinyl. If the music desk is attached to the upper panel, rather than on the inside of the fallboard, the music stays put when you close the instrument. Such desks may extend almost the whole width of the instrument.

Lid

To make the sound of an upright piano a little more direct, you

51

can open the lid. On some pianos, only the front half of the lid opens, so you can leave any objects on top of the back half. Other lids are hinged at the back, and still others (known as *grand-style lids*) are hinged at the side, or in the middle of the lid, so you can open either the left- or the right-hand half.

More volume

To raise the maximum sound level a little and open the sound of the instrument up — which may be handy when playing with a drummer — pianists sometimes take off the entire upper panel. That's easily done and doesn't require any tools. Should the backs of the hammers hit the fallboard, you may remove that part too. However, this does mean losing your music desk and exposing the vulnerable action parts to possible damage.

Different lids: a hinge in the middle, at the back and at the side.

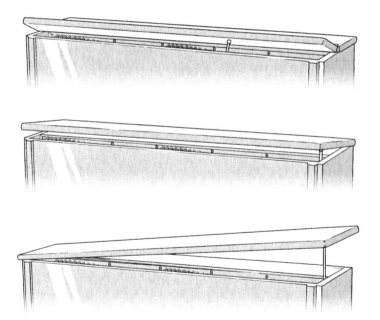

Openings

Some pianos have special openings to make the tone a bit fuller or more direct. These might be located at the back, just under the lid, for instance. Other instruments have part of the upper panel made of cloth, or a kind of grillwork set into the lower panel.

Grand pianos: the front-lid

Many grand pianos have a few small rubber pads glued onto the front lid. These pads prevent the front lid from touching and damaging the main lid when you open it. If there are no pads, you can have them installed or use a (removable) special cushion for the same purpose.

The music desk

The music desk of a grand piano can often be set in three or four different positions. The music shelf, to which it is attached with hinges, can be slid out of the instrument completely to provide access to the tuning pins. Pianists who don't use sheet music sometimes remove the music shelf permanently, which may slightly open up the sound.

Less volume

If you want a grand to produce as little volume as possible, but still want to use the music desk, then remove the music shelf, close the front lid, and position the shelf with the music desk on top of it.

TIP

Main lid

The main lid of a grand can usually be opened in two settings. Occasionally the *lid prop* or *top stick*, which holds it up, allows for three settings. In the lowest setting, the lid is only slightly open. Some grands have a big round knob on the side. This operates a hook that holds the grand's lid in place during (vertical) transportation.

Upright: the back posts

At the back of an upright there are often three to six thick posts that provide extra support. The required number of posts, their thickness, and their location depend mainly on the construction of the rest of the instrument. Some smaller uprights don't have back posts at all. In this case, a heavier frame is used. Building an instrument without back posts is less expensive, and it makes the cabinet around two to four inches (5–10 cm) less deep.

53

The lid and the music desk can always be set in two or more positions.

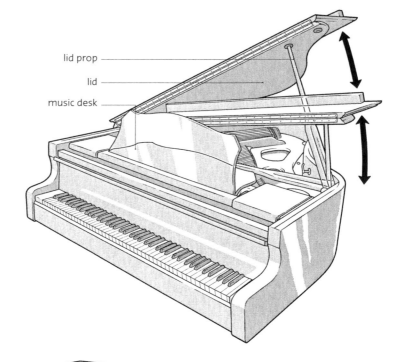

lid prop
lid
music desk

A piano without back posts: The thick vertical posts are missing (see page 10).

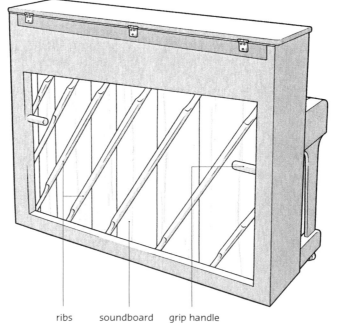

ribs   soundboard   grip handle

Grand piano: braces

The 'back posts' on grand pianos are referred to as *braces*, and they come in all kinds of variations — the *tone collector*, for instance, in which the posts come together at one point. Of course, while it can certainly affect the tone, you shouldn't choose or reject a particular instrument just because of the arrangement of the back posts, nor for the number of posts or the exact dimensions of other components large or small.

Spruce or beech

The type of wood used for the back posts is another subject that has been much discussed. For instance, some experts say posts made of solid spruce promote a warmer tone, whereas mahogany supposedly helps produce a slightly stronger tone. In the end, the type of wood chosen was the one the manufacturer felt suited his instrument the best, whether for reasons of tone, price, or strength, or all three.

Upright cabinet

The panels, lid, and fallboard of an upright piano are traditionally made of laminated wood, usually composed of several plies of poplar or birch. Newer instruments often use MDF (medium-density fiberboard) instead, and for low-budget instruments particle board may be used. It's often impossible to tell exactly which material has been used, as it will be finished by a wood veneer.

Moisture

The use of MDF and similar materials doesn't make for a lower quality instrument per se. In fact, such materials are often

---

Rim

Depending on the design of the instrument, the cabinet (of an upright) itself or the rim (of a grand piano) may influence the tone too. Maple or beech are often used for grand piano rims, and a few makes have rims made of spruce, the same material used for the soundboard.

55

more resistant to warping than solid wood panels. This may be worth taking into account if you are intending to put the piano somewhere where temperature and relative humidity (RH) vary a lot. That said, particle board is typically a lesser quality type of material, and screws can come loose rather easily.

THE KEYBOARD

Most uprights and grand pianos have eighty-eight keys. Older models sometimes have three fewer at the high end, while an occasional, expensive long grand has four or even nine extra keys in the bass register (see page 158). The extra long strings that come with those additional keys contribute to the tone of the entire instrument.

Ivory or synthetic
In the past, white keys were almost always covered with ivory. The synthetic *key covering* that is now mostly used feels a little smoother (more slippery, some would say), but it discolors less quickly and it's easier to maintain. Some brands have synthetic imitation ivory, sporting names such as *ivoplast* or *ivorite*. Other manufacturers cover the keys of particular models with bone or mammoth ivory, from mammoths that have been buried under the Siberian ice for thousands of years.

Ebony or plastic
The black keys or *sharps* are often made of plastic. Only more expensive models and older instruments still have wooden sharps, usually made of ebony. Many pianists prefer wood to plastics because they say it feels better, again, being less slippery.

Balanced
In order to balance out the keys, small pieces of *key lead* are set into them. In uprights they are often placed near the far ends of the keys, where they are invisible from the outside. If they are set into the side of the keys, as in grand pianos, you can sometimes

just about see them if you press down the neighboring keys
completely.

Key dip

In a well-regulated grand piano, the keys can be pressed down
about 0.4" (1 cm). This distance is known as the instrument's *key
dip*.

- If there's **too much** key dip, it takes too long before the
  instrument responds, which makes it harder to play fast,
  technical phrases.

- If there's **too little** key dip, the dynamic range (the difference
  between loud and soft) will be reduced.

- The key dip has to be **the same for each key**, regulated to the
  nearest hundredth of an inch.

Equally high, evenly spaced

On used instruments especially, it's a good idea to check
whether all the keys are at the same height (usually a matter
of proper regulation) and whether there's an even spacing
between all keys. Of course, the keys must not touch each
other at any point.

Long keys, short keys

The keys of a grand piano are slightly longer than those of an
upright, which is one of the reasons why a grand plays differently.
Very short keys, such as the ones on some small pianos, do not
play very easily. The action, which has been adapted to fit the
smaller cabinet, plays a role too.

Keyboards

Rather than make all their own components, most piano
manufacturers buy them at specialized factories. Kluge and
Langer, for instance, are two well-known keyboard makers.
Some piano manufacturers buy all their keyboards from these
companies; others use them only for their top models.

57

Is better-known better?
A tip: Most manufacturers won't use expensive parts by famous makes in a piano that isn't really worth it. On the other hand, a list of prestigious brand names doesn't necessarily mean a piano will sound or play great.

THE ACTION

When you press down a key and let go of it again, you set a whole series of parts in motion. This mechanism, the action, works well only if it's properly regulated — and there are twenty-five or more points of adjustment per key!

Seventy parts
Each key controls an action made up of some sixty or seventy parts, from the *front-rail pin* to the *damper-spring bushing* and the *whippen-flange screw*. Exactly what all of those minor parts do has been described extensively in countless technical piano books, so the information is available if you're interested.

Simultaneously
The action is as complicated as it is because many things have to happen simultaneously or in quick succession: hammer to string, damper off, hammer straight back and ready for the next note, damper back to string, and so on.

Quality
An instrument with a better action plays better, feels better, and lasts longer. Of course, even the best action won't feel good if it isn't properly regulated.

Let-off
One example of a point of adjustment is the *let-off*. If you look inside a piano while very slowly pressing down a key, you'll see that the hammer falls back just before it touches the string. The let-off, also known as *set-off* or *escapement*, is adjusted via the *let-*

off button. This button controls when the jack escapes from under the hammer butt, so that the hammer can fall back.

Tipcode PIANO-009
This Tipcode shows how the hammer falls back right before touching the string, if you press the relevant key down very slowly.

TIPCODE

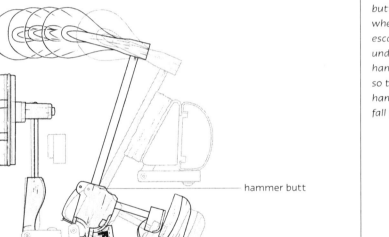

hammer butt

jack

regulating screw

let-off button

The let-off button controls when the jack escapes from under the hammer butt, so that the hammer can fall back.

59

Too soon, too late

If the hammer falls back too soon, you won't hear a thing at all if you play very softly, playing loudly becomes difficult, and even producing a decent sounding note will be tricky. If the adjustment is off in the other direction, the hammer may hit the string twice when you play very softly.

Type of action

Smaller upright pianos have a different type of action, adapted to fit the smaller case. As a result, these instruments may have a different 'feel' than taller pianos. This difference is largest when you compare a spinet to a full-size upright. Spinets and some other small pianos have an *indirect blow action* or *drop action*: The action is mounted below the keys. Taller uprights have a *direct blow action*. All the same, an expensive small piano will typically play (and sound) better than a very low-budget tall one.

Not all the same

Every instrument 'feels' different, regardless of its size. Some have a light touch; others will feel a bit heavier, requiring more power. This is mainly related to the force that is required to press the keys down and the force they come back up with (the *up weight*). A good ratio between the two is important for the repetition speed of the keys.

Touch weight

If you like a solid-feeling keyboard, you're probably more likely to choose an instrument with a fairly high *touch weight*. The touch weight is a combination of the up weight and the *down weight* (the force required to play a soft note).

Figures

The down weight usually varies between 1.6 and 1.95 ounces (45–55 grams); the up weight will typically be between 0.7 and 1.05 ounces (20–30 grams). Of course, playing the instrument will tell you a lot more about it than these numbers ever will.

Lighter or heavier

A piano that plays quite heavily can be adjusted to feel a bit lighter, and vice versa.

Further up the key

Usually, you can best tell how heavy or light the piano feels by playing fast passages. You may also try to feel the difference by playing with your fingers further towards the back of the keys. Some chords automatically force you to do that.

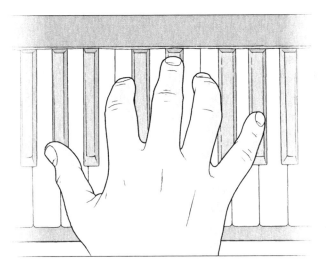

An A-flat major chord: You feel the difference better further up the key.

Even

The bass register keys require a bit more force than the treble keys, because of their heavier hammers. The change from bass to treble should be very gradual, and two neighboring keys may of course not have a different feel to them. Check the feel of the keys by playing fast and slow phrases, loudly and softly, using the entire keyboard.

Unresponsive

On some pianos, you press down a key and, for a split second,

---

Regulate first

If you like the sound and the looks of an instrument, but not the feel, you can ask to have it regulated. Play it again after regulation, before you decide to buy the piano.

TIP

nothing seems to happen. If this is the case, you will also have little control over the tone, and the dynamic range will be limited. This can be a matter of poor regulation, and on used instruments it can be a sign of wear.

Who needs a good action?
Some say that only good pianists need a truly good, quick, responsive action, but even as a novice you will play better if the instrument has a good, well-regulated action, so you'll probably play longer and enjoy it more. Again: If an instrument is only 'good enough to start on,' you may not get much further than starting.

Fast and responsive
On a grand piano, the hammer heads and the dampers simply fall back into place through gravity, when you let go of the keys. That's one of the reasons why a grand piano action feels more responsive and gives you more control over the tone and the dynamics. It also explains why it allows you to repeat notes more quickly, up to twelve times a second: A grand piano key doesn't have to come back up all the way before you can play it again. An upright key does, almost.

Repetition mechanism
That's why, on most uprights, the repetition speed is limited to some eight or nine times a second, assuming you can even play

Up to twelve times a second...

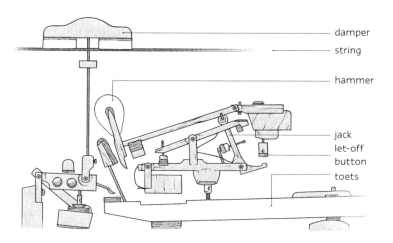

damper
string
hammer
jack
let-off button
toets

that fast. That said, various manufacturers have devised systems to solve this problem. Such systems may work with a special repetition lever (Steingraeber), a set of magnets (SMR, a Dutch invention used by Seiler) or a spring (Sauter's R2 system or Fandrich's Vertical Action).

Standard or optional

Dedicated repetition systems are standard on some makes and optional on others. They usually demand special regulation, and they can be more sensitive to changes in humidity (see page 122 and onwards). You won't usually find them in the lowest or highest price ranges.

Faster

With or without such systems, one piano may repeat faster than the next. Have a look at how far the keys have to come back up before you can use them again; that may tell you what to expect from the instrument you're playing.

All the keys

If you have found an instrument that sounds and feels good, try all the keys one by one. Play them equally hard first, then soft; listen for rattles or buzzes. Also listen to the effect of the dampers. They must stop each note just as quickly and evenly. Please note that

Wood or synthetic?

Synthetic action parts are quite widely used. Mostly in lower-budget models at first, but as their quality has gone up and new materials have been introduced, they can be found in high-end instruments as well. Some of their advantages are that they're more consistent, less sensitive to wear, and to changes in temperature and air humidity. Likewise, the synthetic buckskin that may be used in modern actions lasts longer than natural buckskin. Tip: Some of the synthetic parts used in the 1960s may become brittle. That's something to check, or have checked, if you plan to buy a piano made in that era.

63

the highest fifteen to twenty notes don't have dampers (see pages 64–66).

Tricky legato
Dampers shouldn't leave the string too late, nor must they return too quickly. If strings get muted again too soon, it is very hard to play legato, for instance, where each note has to flow into the next.

Brands
Actions are often built by specialized manufacturers, usually according to the specifications of the piano manufacturer. The best-known name is Renner. A growing number of actions is made in China (e.g., Ningbo Luo, Yumei). Detoa (formerly Tofa) is a Czech action maker.

HAMMERS AND DAMPERS

For a piano to sound, good it needs good hammer heads and precisely-regulated hammers. The same goes for the dampers.

Large heads
To set the long, thick bass strings in motion, you need big, heavy hammer heads, and pianos have equally big dampers to mute them. As you go up the keyboard, both hammer heads and dampers become gradually smaller.

Bass strings require larger hammers and dampers.

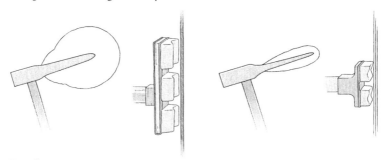

No dampers
The strings of the highest one-and-a-half octaves vibrate so briefly

that they don't need a damper at all. On most pianos, the last damper is somewhere between E6 and A6 (see page 18). The first key without a damper can be easily located: Simply play short notes in that area, key by key going upwards, until you hear the first note that goes on sounding when you let go of the key.

Tipcode PIANO-010
You can easily tell the difference between the last strings with a damper, and the first strings without, as demonstrated in this Tipcode.

TIPCODE

As small as possible

The difference should not be too striking, but you can always clearly hear the difference between the last note with a damper, and the first note without. To limit the difference in tone and sustain, the last damper typically muffles its unison very lightly.

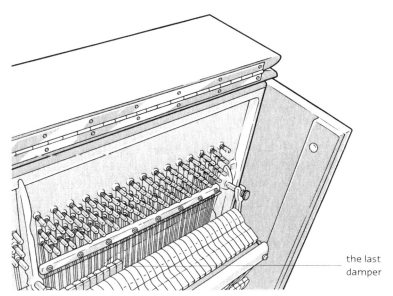

the last damper

The highest-sounding strings don't use dampers.

65

Richer

If the instrument is tuned well, the upper octave and a half
contribute to a richer, fuller sounding instrument: The damperless
strings resonate along with every note you play.

Just as high, just as far

On a well-regulated upright, the hammers are all at the same
position along the strings. If a hammer strikes a string at a higher
or lower point than it should, that note will sound noticeably
different from the rest, especially in the higher treble area. All
hammers must also be equally far from the strings: Uneven
hammer strokes result in uneven dynamics.

Touch or jam

The hammers should be evenly spaced. If hammers are too close
together or do not move in a straight line, there's a chance that
they will touch or even jam when you're playing. Also, a crooked
hammer won't hit the string properly.

TIP

An extra string

*Especially on very small uprights, a hammer may graze a
string from the next note along. To check for this, press
the damper pedal and play note for note, very slowly, while
listening carefully to each tone.*

Voicing

For a good tone, the felt hammer heads should have the right
hardness. If they're too hard, the tone will be harsh or edgy.
Hammers that are too soft will make for a dullish tone, lacking
brightness. The process of making hammers harder or softer is
called voicing (see page 135).

Only so far

As it's not just the hammer heads that determine the tone, voicing
a piano cannot completely alter the sound of the instrument. Want
to know more? Turn to the buying tips for pre-owned instruments

on pages 83–77, and read the sections on tuning and regulation (pages 129 and 135 respectively).

Edgy
Voicing takes time. If it hasn't been done properly, a piano may start to sound noticeably harsher or edgier even after just a few months. Ultimately, every piano needs to be re-voiced.

Heavy felt
Some brochures mention exactly how heavy the felt of the hammer heads is. On their own, such figures once again tell you little: The 'best' felt weight depends very much on the design of the whole instrument.

Brands
Abel, Renner, Ronsen, and Imadegawa are some of the best-known hammer head makers.

STRINGS

Both uprights and grand pianos have around two hundred and twenty strings. Of course, all strings must be evenly spaced across the instrument — but there is more to see and to know than that.

Twenty-five feet
Of the thinnest, highest strings, usually only a section of two or three inches (5–8 cm) actually vibrates. If the longest bass string were equally thin, it could only sound as low as it should if it were a good twenty or twenty-five feet long (7–8 meters).

Wound
This explains why these strings are a good deal thicker. The extra mass allows them to sound low enough without becoming too long. Lower sounding strings use heavier-gauge string wire, and the lowest strings are also wound with copper wire, in two or even three layers, adding extra mass to the strings.

67

The grouping of the strings in a grand piano. The mechanics are virtually the same in an upright.

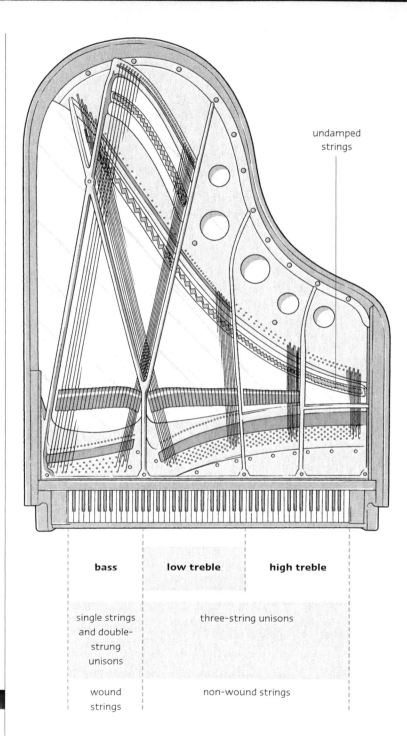

undamped strings

bass	low treble	high treble
single strings and double-strung unisons	three-string unisons	
wound strings	non-wound strings	

Single, double, and triple strings

The very lowest notes have only one string each. The higher-sounding bass notes are two-string unisons: Each hammer strikes two strings at once. In the treble area there are three non-wound (*plain*) steel strings for each note.

Transition

Going from the bass strings to the low treble, three things change: The lower treble strings run across a different bridge, they are not wound, and there are three of them for each note. To make this transition as smooth as possible, the low treble section often starts with a few double-wound string unisons.

Listen

If the transition is really smooth, no note sounds noticeably fuller, warmer, or less bright than the one next to it. A tip for listening: Play the area where the number of strings per key change, note for note, very softly, and don't look at the strings. If you do, you may easily end up hearing what you see.

Scale

The word *scale* may refer to only the *speaking length* of the strings (the part that actually vibrates), but often it is also used as a general term for the precise number, gauge, and winding of the strings, and everything directly connected to it. In a piano featuring a *German scale design* the stringing is based on a German design. This tells you nothing about the quality of the instrument, however. The illustration on the opposite page shows you roughly how the strings are grouped.

Replacing strings

Do you want to get the best from your instrument? After about twenty or thirty years, strings will have lost some of their tone and brightness, so you may have them replaced. On most pianos, strings are replaced only after fifty years or more. Grand pianos in concert halls get new strings more often.

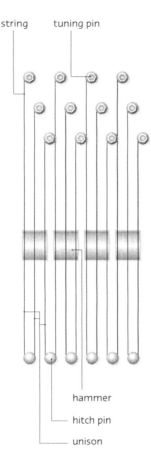

string   tuning pin

hammer

hitch pin

unison

Loop strung

The three-string unisons are usually *loop strung*: One end of each length of string is fixed to a tuning pin, looped around the hitch pin and then fixed to the next tuning pin. In other words, one string length makes two of the unison's strings.

Single stringing

There are only a few (expensive) brands that have three separate strings for a three-string unison. This is fairly easy to check on an open grand piano. If it has , each string is tied to the hitch pin.

String wire

The string wires are nearly always made in specialized factories. Well-known makes include Giese, Mapes (US), Poehlman, and Röslau (Germany). Winding the bass strings, on the other hand, is something many piano makers do in house.

Round, hexagonal, or octagonal

The cores of the wound strings may be either round, or six- or eight-sided (hexagonal or octagonal, respectively). The difference can be clearly seen and felt along the non-wound ends of these strings. Hexagonal and octagonal cores are said to make the winding easier and longer-lasting, while reducing the risk of noise;

TIP

From thick to thin

The thickest strings are easily six or seven times as thick as the thinnest, and your lowest bass strings can be twenty to thirty (!) times as long as your shortest treble strings.

other experts claim that round core strings promote a fuller tone, for example. The truth? You'll find both types in both expensive and lower budget instruments — and again, in the end it's how the whole instrument sounds that counts.

Tension

String tension is another parameter. Some makers apply higher string tensions than others. The construction of the instrument and the choice of strings play a role too. As an example, a relatively low string tension is said to give a more singing, sustained tone, while a high-tension scale would make for a brighter sound. Some experts also state that strings sound their best if they're as tight as can be, without breaking — and others disagree.

PINS, BLOCKS, AND BRIDGES

The strings run from the tuning pins to the hitch pins. On the way they pass not only the bridge, which transmits the vibrations to the soundboard, but also the pressure bar or a number of agraffes.

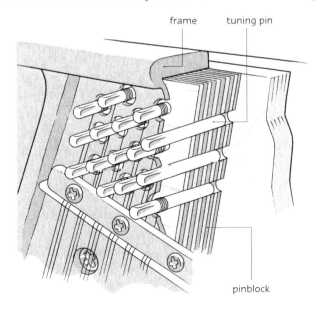

frame   tuning pin

pinblock

The pinblock is hidden behind the frame.

71

Pinblock

The pinblock, because it holds the tuning pins, has to take a whole lot of tension. That's why it's made up of laminated hardwood, the number of plies varying from three to thirty or more. This number doesn't say a thing about the quality of the block or the instrument. You'll find pinblocks with any number of plies in all price ranges. Solid pinblocks can be found in older instruments.

Makes

Well-known pinblock manufacturers are Delignit and Dehonit, both from Germany. There are also piano manufacturers who make their own pinblocks. The quality of the pinblock is one the main elements that influence the tuning stability of the instrument.

Slightly upwards

In order to withstand the tension of the strings, the tuning pins or *wrest pins* usually point slightly upward in an upright piano, and slightly towards the player in a grand. There must be some space between the string and the frame; only then can the string be tightened further if necessary.

A good pinblock

If the tuning pins are not all set at the same angle, or if some pins have obviously been hit deeper into the block, there may be something wrong with the pinblock or *wrest block*. Also, on a well-made piano, the tuning pins are set far enough apart that the strings don't touch each other at any point.

Bridges

A violin has a small, thin wooden bridge, which transmits the vibrations of the strings to the top of the instrument, which amplifies and colors the sound. Pianos work in just the same way, on that point at least: Two bridges pass on the vibrations to the soundboard, which sets the surrounding air in motion, producing sound. There's a separate short bridge for the bass strings; all other strings use the *treble bridge* or *long bridge*.

Bridge pins

The better the contact between bridge and strings, the better the result will be. That's why the strings run zigzag across the bridge, kept in place by the *bridge pins*. These small metal pins also help to transmit the vibrations.

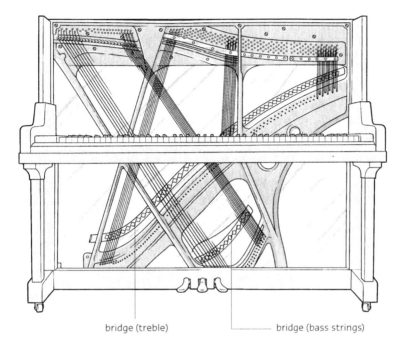

The bridges transmit the vibrations of the strings to the soundboard...

bridge (treble)   bridge (bass strings)

bridge

... just like a violin bridge transmits the vibrations of the strings to the body.

Pressure bar

From the tuning pins, the strings either run under a metal *pressure bar*, or through small brass studs, known as *agraffes*. The agraffes, having one hole per string length, ensure that the strings are spaced at the right distance from each other.

73

Agraffes

Almost all grand pianos have agraffes for the bass strings and the low treble, and a pressure bar for the high treble. On upright pianos you find almost all combinations in almost all price ranges — agraffes throughout, a pressure bar for all the strings, or perhaps agraffes only for the bass strings. In other words, the use of agraffes or pressure bars says nothing about the quality or price of the instrument.

Agraffes for the bass strings, and a pressure bar for the higher-sounding strings.

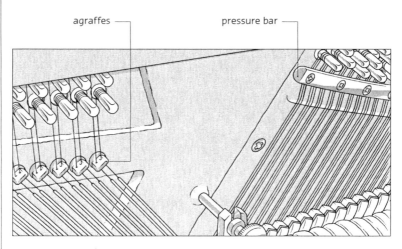

agraffes —   pressure bar —

The ends

The speaking length of the strings does not include the string ends (i.e., the sections near the tuning pins at one end, and at the hitch pins at the other). Even so, these sections do vibrate along, very softly. That can be disturbing, especially on the lower strings. The sound is usually suppressed with felt.

Duplex scale

In many grand pianos, however, the end parts of the higher-sounding strings are used to enhance the tone. With the help of small metal 'ridges', these sections are adjusted so that they are in tune with the actual speaking lengths of the strings. This is a Steinway invention, called *duplex scale*.

Less bright

You can easily hear how important those vibrations at the ends of

74

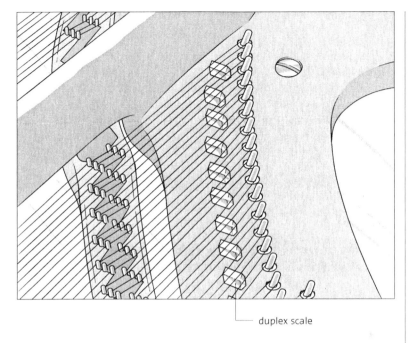

duplex scale

A *duplex scale with small adjustable combs for each unison* (Estonia).

the strings are. First play a note, then put a finger to muffle the end part of the appropriate string, and play the note again. It'll sound less bright the second time.

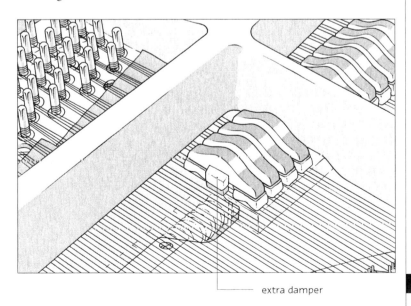

extra damper

Aliquot scale: four strings per unison. Each damper has a small extra damper attached for the fourth string (Bluthner).

75

Aliquot scale

The German company Blüthner has another method to enhance the sound of the highest octaves: All three-string unisons have a fourth string added. This string is not struck by the hammer, but if you play quite loudly, it does vibrate along sympathetically. The name of this *aliquot scale* comes from the French *son aliquot*, which means *harmonic* or *overtone*.

SOUNDBOARD

The soundboard is often referred to as the soul or the voice of the instrument. Usually, this large wooden plate is made up of thin planks of spruce. It is no coincidence that this is the same type of wood used for the tops of violins and many guitars.

Grain

For a good tone, the vibrations need to be able to pass through the whole soundboard very quickly. Vibrations move fastest if the wood has a fine, straight grain. For this purpose, trees should grow slowly. Wood used for soundboards comes from Northern Italy, Germany, Eastern Europe, Alaska, and other regions.

Crown

The soundboard isn't perfectly flat. On a grand, its center rises up about a third of an inch; on an upright it curves slightly toward the keyboard. This curve, called the *crown* or *belly*, keeps the wood under tension, which contributes to the tone.

Ribs

The ribs on the soundboard are perpendicular to the grain of the wood. This helps to distribute the vibrations across the soundboard faster. The ribs also help maintain the soundboard's shape.

A bit flatter

After many years, most soundboards do get a bit flatter, and that can make the tone a bit flatter too. On the other hand: However important the crown is, there are plenty of instruments, old and new, that sound excellent but have no crown at all, or one that is barely noticeable.

Cracks

The forces on the soundboard can not only flatten it in time, but it may crack too. This can even occur very rapidly if the wood shrinks or expands a lot, for instance, if it is exposed to rapid changes in temperature or humidity. Eventually, after half a century or more, just about every soundboard will develop cracks. Fortunately, in most cases the piano's performance will not suffer from them. There's more about cracked soundboards — and how to prevent them — on page 122, and on page 87 and onwards.

From thick to thin

Most soundboards are about a third of an inch (1 cm) thick at the high treble, where they preferably show a very fine grain. That makes the wood a bit stiffer, which in turn helps the highest frequencies to sound good. At the side of the bass strings, the soundboard is often a little thinner with a coarser grain, which enhances the lower frequencies. All kinds of ideas have been developed to help soundboards to 'sing.' For instance, there are soundboards with a groove around them, which supposedly allows them to vibrate more freely.

Bigger? Maybe not...

Larger instruments can sound 'bigger' because they have a bigger soundboard, among other reasons. You can't always tell from the outside, however. Some manufacturers make vertical pianos with a tall cabinet that houses a relatively small soundboard, for instance. Conversely, some companies make their grands a bit wider, which allows for a slightly larger soundboard than other instruments of equal length.

Laminated soundboards

Instead of a soundboard made of solid planks of wood, many instruments have a laminated one. The earliest laminated soundboards were mostly used in low-budget pianos, but today,

77

you may also find them in higher quality instruments. That said, the best instruments still feature solid wood. Laminated soundboards have more advantages than their lower production costs: They are very resistant to changes in humidity and temperature, and they don't crack or go flat.

How to tell

You can often tell a laminated soundboard by looking at the grain of the wood. First take a look at back of the piano, then peek inside the instrument. If the grain on the outside runs in a different direction, you're looking at laminated wood. The same is true when the grain runs straight down rather than diagonally. If there's a hole in the soundboard, a look at the edge of the hole will tell you if it's solid wood or plywood.

PEDALS

Most uprights and grand pianos have three pedals. Only the one on the right is identical on both instruments.

Damper pedal

The right-hand pedal is called the sustain(ing) pedal because it allows the strings to sustain by lifting all the dampers

TIPCODE

Tipcode PIANO-011
This Tipcode shows you how the damper pedal lifts all of the dampers off of the strings.

78

simultaneously. This explains why it's also known as the *damper pedal*.

Different sound

When you use this pedal, the timbre of the instruments changes too, as the strings of the keys you don't play vibrate along softly with everything you do play. Play the chord shown below and keep the keys pressed down a little while. Let them go. Now press down the sustain pedal, then play the same thing. You'll hear the difference.

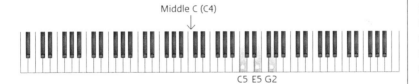

Middle C (C4)

C5 E5 G2

Play long notes: first without, then with the sustain pedal.

At the same time

When you press the damper pedal, check whether all the dampers leave the strings at the same time. If you use this pedal a lot, you're likely to keep your foot resting on it lightly. For this reason, the dampers mustn't respond immediately, but only when you press the pedal down a little further.

Well-regulated pedal

A well-regulated damper pedal allows you to control the dampers very precisely, moving them to and from the strings as fast or as slowly as the music requires.

TIP

Noise

When checking out a piano, listen for unwanted noise when operating the pedals. For example, play a chord loudly with the sustain pedal pressed down, and then let the pedal come back up very slowly. Are all the notes damped equally and at the same time? Are there any rattles, buzzes, or squeaks?

79

Soft pedal

The soft pedal of an upright piano, on the left-hand side, is also known as the *half-blow pedal*: Moving the hammers closer to the strings reduces the hammer stroke ('half blow') and thus the sound potential of the instrument.

A different feel

Using the soft pedal makes the piano sound a bit softer, but it will feel slightly different as well. As the hammers move towards the strings, a tiny bit of space opens up above the jack (see the illustration on page 59). This space has to be bridged before the hammer is set in motion. As a result, the keyboard will be less responsive, and your control over the tone will be reduced. The effect is worse on some instruments than on others.

The middle pedal

The middle pedal of an upright is often a muffler pedal, also known as the practice pedal, *mute pedal, celeste pedal*, and *moderator stop*. It lowers a strip of felt between the hammers and the strings, which substantially reduces the volume. Unfortunately, it also makes the instrument feel quite different, as the felt changes the rebound of the hammers.

TIPCODE

Tipcode PIANO-003
Depressing the practice pedal lowers a muffling strip of felt between the hammers and the strings.

Locked

Most practice pedals can be locked in the 'on' position, either by moving the pedal a little to the left when pressing it down, or by simply pressing it down once. (Pressing it down once more will release the pedal.)

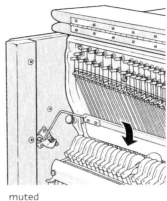

A strip of felt between hammers and strings...

not muted   muted

By hand

There are hand-operated versions as well. Most of these models have a lever, usually hidden under the keyboard. The most basic versions require you to open the lid to lower or raise the felt. These types of mufflers can rather easily be retrofit into most upright pianos. Practice mutes on grands are very rare.

Mute rail

The middle pedal can have other functions too. If the piano has a sound module, the pedal may be used to lower a rubber clad bar or rail. This *mute rail* or *hammer-stop* rail stops the hammers right before they would hit the strings. This allows you to practice in complete silence (Hybrid pianos; see Chapter 7). Many instruments have either a mute rail or a muffler; some have both, one being operated with a lever, the other with a pedal.

Tipcode PIANO-012
This Tipcode demonstrates the effect of a mute rail. It catches the hammers right before they can hit the strings, allowing for silent practice.

TIPCODE

81

Bass sustain

On some instruments the middle pedal lifts the dampers in the bass register only. Such a *bass sustain pedal* is only really useful if all the notes you want to sustain happen to be in the bass, which is rarely the case.

Grands and lyres

The lyre is the part of a grand piano that holds the pedals. On some grands, it actually has the shape of a lyre.

A lyre-shaped lyre.

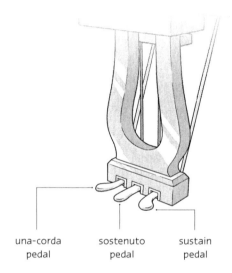

una-corda   sostenuto   sustain
pedal   pedal   pedal

The una-corda pedal

The left-hand pedal of a grand piano is known the as una-corda pedal. The name, una corda ('one string'), stems from the early days of the instrument, when it had two strings for each note. Of those two, only one was struck if you used the una-corda pedal.

One less, one more

When you press the una-corda pedal, the hammers should move far enough to the side so that they really do strike one less string in each unison, without grazing one of the strings of the neighboring unison. If you press down the keys very slowly one by one, you can clearly see whether the hammers are striking where they should. If you listen closely, you can hear it too.

82

The sostenuto pedal

Nearly all modern grand pianos have a sostenuto pedal (see page 17); many older models don't. Does that matter? There isn't much music that requires this third pedal. It is used in some works of Johann Sebastian Bach, which is why some refer to it as the *Bach pedal*. Another name is a *Steinway pedal*. The company acquired the patent on the original sostenuto pedal, which was invented by Pleyel in 1875.

Tipcode PIANO-007
This Tipcode demonstrates the effect of a sostenuto pedal.

TIPCODE

Uprights and sostenuto pedals

Some uprights can be ordered with a sostenuto pedal for an additional charge. On old instruments you may come across a *bass sostenuto*, which obviously works only in the lowest register.

Four pedals

The Italian company Fazioli makes grands with a fourth pedal. This *pianississimo pedal* works just about the same way as the soft pedal of an upright piano, yet without its disadvantages (see page 80).

JUDGING PRE-OWNED PIANOS

It's hard to properly judge a pre-owned piano. Even so, there are all kinds of things you can check for yourself, in addition to what was discussed above, before reaching the point where you need to

83

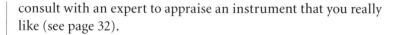
consult with an expert to appraise an instrument that you really
like (see page 32).

Play, look and listen

When you are playing, listen out especially for rattles or buzzes,
watch out for keys that are hard work to play, or that creak or
squeak, and for hammers that double-strike when you play softly.
Feel to check that there are no keys that can move sideways too
easily. The greatest wear is usually in the middle part of the
keyboard. That's where pianos get played the most.

Very light

If a piano plays very, very easily, this may indicate excessive wear,
lack of regulation, or both: The action of a badly regulated piano
will wear faster. If either one is the case, it will usually be hard
or impossible to play really softly, the volume will be difficult to
control, and the action will probably be noisy.

Inside

Have a look inside too. Ask the person selling the piano to remove
lamps, vases, and other items from the instrument, and to open the
lid. This reduces the risk of breaking or damaging things yourself.

Hammers

Check whether all the hammers of an upright are spaced evenly,
lined up and at equal distances from the strings (see page 66).
Hold down different groups of keys and look to see whether the
hammers stay in line. When you let the keys go, the hammers
should all fall back at the same time.

Heads with grooves

Grooves in the hammer heads are normal on a pre-owned piano.
Look very carefully at the hammer heads in the middle section of
the instrument. They usually have the most to put up with. The
grooves should never be near the edge of the head, but roughly in
the middle. The strings should fall exactly into those grooves. You
can check this by pressing the keys down very softly, and holding
them down. This allows you to see where the hammers hit the
strings.

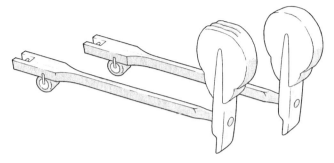

*A worn-out
hammer head
with deep
grooves, and
a new head.*

Deep grooves and moths

If the grooves are very deep, the hammer heads can be sanded
back into shape, provided that felt is still thick enough and hasn't
dried out too much. Take another look at the hammers, as moths
have a taste for felt! Replacing hammer heads easily costs nine
hundred dollars or more.

Strings

*Rusty strings? If so, the piano may have been kept in a very
damp room. That can be a problem if you move it to a house
with low air humidity (see page 122). Rust also causes a dull
tone, and rusty strings are harder to tune. If you find a couple
of new strings between a whole bunch of old ones, it can be a
sign that more strings are going to break.*

Properly tuned

Just like a new piano, you can only judge a pre-owned piano if it's
properly tuned. If a piano is flat (too low) over the whole range, it
won't sound out of tune by itself, but playing with other musicians
may be problematic. Besides, a piano sounds best when tuned to
the right pitch. Last but not least, a piano that sounds a half-step
or more too low usually can't be tuned back up to the right pitch
with one tuning (see page 131). So how can you check the general
pitch?

A=440

Pianos should be tuned so that the strings of A4 (see page 17) vibrate
440 times per second. This is known as A=440 hertz or A=440.

Tuning fork

An affordable way to check this is to use a tuning fork. This is a small, metal, two-pronged fork that sounds a very clear pitch. Tuning forks, available for a few dollars, come in various pitches. Get one that is labeled A=440. Tap the tuning fork against your knee and hold the stem against the cabinet or against your ear. Play A4 and compare the two pitches. If the piano sounds higher or lower, it needs to be tuned. If it sounds way lower, it may need a double tuning or pitch raising (again, see page 131).

(again, see page 131)

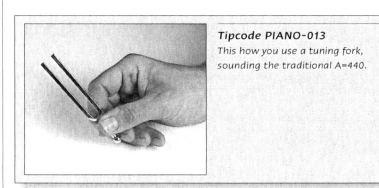

Tipcode PIANO-013
This how you use a tuning fork, sounding the traditional A=440.

A tuning fork.

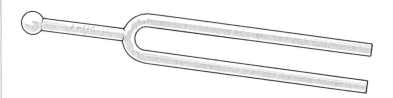

Tuner

You can use an electronic tuner instead. The built-in microphone 'hears' the pitch, and a series of LEDs or a pointer tells you whether the tone is in tune, flat, or sharp. Electronic tuners are available for some twenty to thirty dollars. *Tip*: Most guitarists have one, if you don't.

An expert eye

Judging the condition of important wooden parts (soundboard, pinblock, bridges) and the action requires an expert eye, unless the damage is so bad that you can see it too. Check that the tuning pins are all at the same angle, that the ribs are touching the soundboard all along their length, and that they are not cracked. Should the soundboard need to be replaced, it's worth knowing that such an operation easily costs as much as a decent new piano — and that you can still play an instrument with one or more visible soundboard cracks. Crooked panels? Then there's a good chance that the soundboard is no longer in shape.

Woodworm

Small holes in the wood? That could be woodworm. Woodworms don't like music, so if a piano is played often, it's probably not inhabited.

Overdamper

If you come across a vertical piano that has dampers above the hammers, you can assume it's probably over a hundred years old. Don't spend too much money on this type of piano, known as an *overdamper* (a.k.a. *bird-cage action*).

Straight-strung

Another type to be wary of is the *straight-strung upright*, on which the strings run vertically. Such pianos are usually very old and not worth much. Exceptions are some uprights by Rippen. This Dutch piano manufacturer has been making straight-strung instruments up until the 1980s.

Age

If you want to know exactly how old an instrument is, you can find tables with serial numbers and year of construction for nearly all makes in the *Pierce Piano Atlas* and similar books. Many piano stores have a copy you can consult. Similar lists can be found online as well (see page 000; e.g., *Blue Book Of Pianos*). The serial number is often shown on the frame, but it may be under the lid, on the pinblock, or on the soundboard as well. A tip: Some components have their own serial or other numbers too, so make sure you pick the right one.

6

Auditioning Pianos

This chapter focuses on choosing an instrument by ear, with tips for beginer players, even if you can't really play yet; how to hear the difference between one instrument and the next; and tips that will help you listen more consciously.

In a store, everything sounds different than it does at home. If you ask the salesperson to first let you hear a very bright sounding piano, followed by one with a mellow, warm sound, you'll get an idea of how different instruments can sound in the acoustics of the store. The prices of those instruments are not the point right now.

Start with the extremes
These two extremes are also a good starting point if you don't yet have a clear idea of the sound you're looking for. Decide which of the two appeals to you most, and carry on from there. Another tip: You can also play (or get someone to play) the most affordable and the most expensive piano in the store right after each other, or try one model in each price range. That may give you a better picture of the price-related differences between instruments, and of what you can and should listen out for.

Your own piano
Another starting point is the instrument you already have, if you do. Some piano salespeople will come to your home, to see and hear the room where the instrument will be played in, and to check out the instrument you are currently playing, and its value.

Loud or soft
An instrument sounds much louder and brighter in a room with hard acoustics (wooden floor, little furniture) than in a room with thick rugs and curtains. You need to take that into account when making a choice. The tone can be adjusted slightly (voicing), but don't expect anyone to turn a piano with a decidedly bright tone into a very warm, romantic-sounding instrument.

Impressive
Many piano stores have quite hard acoustics, in which instruments tend to sound quite impressive even if you are a half-decent pianist, especially if you use the sustain pedal a lot and open the lid wide.

Someone else
Most piano salespeople know how to play the instrument. Even so, if you haven't been playing very long yourself, it can be a good idea to take another pianist along on one of your visits — preferably

one who can play what you would like to play yourself, and most importantly someone who will show you what the *piano* can do, rather than what *they* can do.

Quite wrong

Even if you do play, taking a second pianist along can't do any harm. Then you can get the other person to play, so that you can concentrate on listening better. Or you can let that other person play without you seeing which instrument they are playing. If you do, you may find you are quite wrong about which piano you think you are listening to.

Comparing instruments

Choosing instruments on their tone and timbre is primarily a question of comparing. The first piano you play may sound great straightaway — but often you'll only really be able to judge if you play a couple of other instruments right afterwards.

At home

If you are buying at somebody's home, there's nothing to compare the piano with. This makes it even more important to take another player along.

PLAYING

If you sit down to play in a store, try not to wonder what the staff thinks of your playing. If things are good, they don't listen to *how* you play but to *what* you play, in order to be of as much help as possible in choosing an instrument that suits you.

Briefly

If you have a lot of pianos to choose from, it may be best to start by playing only briefly on each instrument. Once you have narrowed

91

down your choice to a manageable number of pianos, compare them two by two or three by three. Discard the one you like least and choose another in its place. And so on. Naturally, you'll want to play longer when you're down to fewer instruments.

Simple

To start with, play simple things. If you don't you'll be focusing more on the notes you should play than on listening to the instrument. Even just scales and chords can give a good first impression.

Even if you can't play

The chords shown below will give you a fair impression of how a piano sounds. Even if you don't really play, you can play them. After all, playing a chord is no more than playing a few keys at the same time. To begin with, choose one of the three chords and play only the keys with the black dots. If you're more than a novice, then play the keys with the white dots too. These three chords

Three great-sounding test chords. Either play the keys with the black dots only, or include the other keys as well.

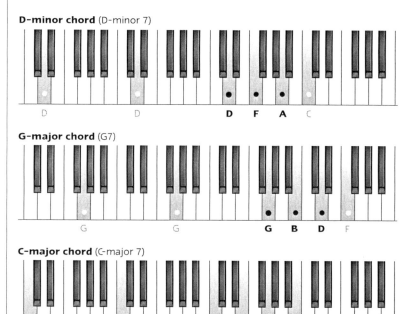

D-minor chord (D-minor 7)

G-major chord (G7)

C-major chord (C-major 7)

will sound best if you play them in the order shown, one after the other.

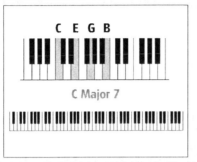

Tipcode PIANO-014
Play this Tipcode to listen to the three chords listed on the opposite page.

TIPCODE

Long notes
Very short notes often tell you less about the tone of an instrument than long notes. Play both.

High, middle, and low
Another simple playing and listening tip: Play the same three-

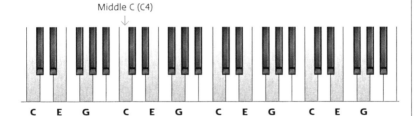

Middle C (C4)

C E G   C E G   C E G   C E G

One chord, played along the entire keyboard (C-major).

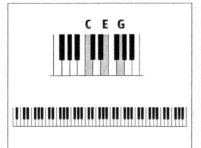

Tipcode PIANO-015
Play his Tipcode to listen to a chord played over the entire range of the piano.

TIPCODE

note chord at different places on the keyboard. Start off high and go down from there, or the other way around, or both. Also, play it loud and soft, sustain the notes or play them very shortly (staccato).

Same chord, different instrument
A variation: Take that same chord and play it on the same keys, but on different pianos. If you try putting what you hear into words, the differences may be easier to remember. Think of words like velvety or bright, warm, full, mellow, transparent, solid, nasal, rich, thin, or shrill — or think in colors. One piano may sound 'browner' to you, another one may have a shade of blue, for example.

Color
Pianists often talk about color in a different way too. The better the instrument is, the more (tonal) colors or timbres it allows you to play, provided you play well enough.

Play longer
You'll naturally want to play longer on those instruments from which you are going to make your final choice. Listening is easiest if you play pieces you know well. Try to play a wide variety of things, from loud to soft, with and without pedals, and from as fast as you can to notes that last a minute each.

Empty music desk
If you are used to playing from sheet music, take some pieces with you when you go to choose a piano. An empty music desk can make playing really hard.

LISTENING

You can't learn how to listen just by reading about it, but you can read about what to listen for.

Even progression

Of course the high notes on a piano sound different than the low notes, but the progression should be very even. Nor should the transitions be too large, for instance from the bass notes to the low treble (page 68), or from the high notes with dampers to the ones without (pages 64–65).

Soft and loud

On a good piano you can play very softly and still get what you want from every note. You can also play very loudly without the sound distorting or becoming metallic or thinnish, or the notes — mainly in the lower register — blurring together so that no one can really hear what you're playing anymore. An instrument that can do all this has good dynamics.

A larger dynamic range than an upright.

95

Louder and brighter

As you start playing harder, the instrument not only starts sounding louder, but brighter too. The degree and evenness of that change differs between instruments.

Try a grand too

Grand pianos generally have a bigger dynamic range than uprights. You can make a grand sound both softer and louder. Choosing an upright? Try listening to what a good grand piano can do too, just so you know what's the maximum you can expect from an instrument.

The lower notes

The differences in character between different instruments often is most obvious in the lowest octaves. Keep playing the same chord in the same lower octave, equally loudly or softly, on different instruments.

Every note

In the very lowest range, check that every separate note stands out, even if you play fast phrases. Also, in a good instrument you can almost feel the bass notes, and a good low note doesn't drone. It produces a beautiful sound.

High

The highest notes always sound short, but they should still sing. 'Plink' is not enough. Good pianos have bright, full-sounding

TIP

Singing

The difference between a piano that can 'sing' and one that can't is quite easy to hear. If you play a chord or two notes at once on a good instrument and keep the keys pressed down, you'll often notice that the sound seems to start singing just after you play the keys, as though the notes are reinforcing each other. You can hear this effect most clearly in the lower range of the piano, highs. Lesser instruments may sound edgy, shrill, or thin in the high treble area.

Middle
The low treble is the range that you'll use the most. It's also the area where pianos tend to sound very much alike. But when you're really playing, you'll certainly hear the difference between one instrument and the next, even within that range.

The attack
It's also important to listen to what happens at the very moment the hammers strike the strings. Much of the difference in tone between one instrument and the next lies in that sound, the *attack*. The attack can be very bright, or it can be soft, warm, mushy, firm, indistinct, aggressive, and so on.

Bright or warm
Pianists often divide pianos into two large groups: the bright-sounding instruments on the one hand, warm-sounding ones on the other. Asian-built pianos are usually placed in the first category, European instruments in the second, and American pianos somewhere in between. However, there may be as many exceptions to this rule as there are pianos, or pianists.

Taste
When two people listen to the same piano, they'll often use very different words to describe what they hear. What one finds shrill (and so not attractive), another may describe as bright (and so not unattractive), and what's warm and romantic to one ear sounds dull or lifeless to another. It all depends on what you like, and on the words that are used to describe what's being heard.

Style
What you like often coincides with what you play. Jazz musicians often choose a brighter-sounding instrument, for example. A thundering, heavily orchestrated piece may sound better on one piano, and something airy and fast better on another; and a large choir may require a different piano sound than a salsa band. In other words, there's no such thing as the best piano.

97

7

Hybrid, Player, and Digital Pianos

Digital technique allows you to play a regular piano in complete silence, to hook pianos up to a computer, or to have pianos play by themselves. An introduction to the possibilities, from sound modules and effects to MIDI.

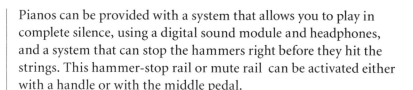
Pianos can be provided with a system that allows you to play in complete silence, using a digital sound module and headphones, and a system that can stop the hammers right before they hit the strings. This hammer-stop rail or mute rail can be activated either with a handle or with the middle pedal.

Silent or hybrid

An instrument with these features can be played both acoustically, as you play any piano, or digitally, activating the stop rail and the sound module. This explains their name, hybrid pianos. Another popular name, silent piano, is self-explanatory.

TIPCODE

Tipcode PIANO-012
In a hybrid piano, you can stop the hammers from hitting the strings by activating a mute rail or hammer-stop rail, as shown in this Tipcode.

Names

Many piano brands have their own silent system. Their trade names often describe their purpose: Anytime, City Piano, DuoVox, Night & Day, MIDIPiano (formerly known as Silent Piano), StillAcoustic, QuietTime, and VARIO System are some examples. Silent system typically cost an extra two thousand dollars or more. The exact price depends, for one thing, on the features of the sound module.

Just like an acoustic

The sound modules that come with such systems are designed to faithfully reproduce the performance of the 'real', acoustic instrument. The volume goes up if you play harder, and the other way around; the pedals have the same effect and feel, and so on. The main differences are that the sound doesn't come from the strings and the soundboard. Instead, you're using a pair of headphones, connected to the instrument's sound module. The keys you play will trigger samples (digital recordings) of the same keys of an acoustic piano. These samples are stored in the module.

Optical sensors

To trigger the samples, the movements of the keys you play are picked up by sensors. Usually these are optical sensors, one under each key, which respond to minute light beams, as this type of sensor doesn't affect the feel of the piano. However, the keyboard will feel slightly different when the mute rail has been activated; the hammers travel less far than when they *do* hit the strings.

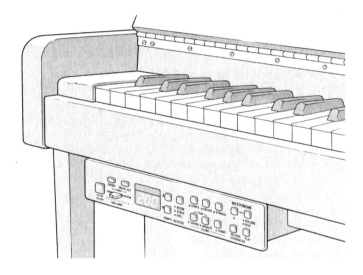

A sound module with extensive options.

Simple

The most basic sound modules have only a volume control and one or two headphone outputs. Having two headphone outputs is handy for lessons or playing duets.

More sounds

More elaborate models usually offer more sounds. Besides samples of one or more grand pianos or uprights, they may feature electric pianos, a few organs, a harpsichord, a choir, or a set of violins (strings). Other modules offer you a choice of hundreds of different instruments or voices.

101

TIPCODE

Tipcode PIANO-016
Next to one or more upright and grand piano sounds, most sound modules also provide samples of the voices demonstrated in this Tipcode: two electrical pianos, a piano with strings, and an organ.

Piano sounds

In the end, most pianists use mainly the 'acoustic' piano voices, or just one of them. So pay special attention to the quality of those sounds, just as you would listen to acoustic pianos. There can be considerable differences between different sound modules.

Metronome

If a metronome is featured on the module, it is helpful if it has a volume control. Most metronomes can accent the first beat of each bar. If so, check if the metronome can also handle odd time signatures (e.g., $\frac{5}{4}$).

Effects

Most modules have one or more built-in digital effects to enhance the sound of the instrument. The most common effect is a *reverb*, which breathes life and space into digital piano sounds. Sound modules that feature samples of other instruments as well

TIPCODE

Tipcode PIANO-017
Some common effects on digital pianos are reverb, chorus, wah-wah, flanger, and delay.

typically provide you with a larger choice of effects. A *chorus*, for example, is a type of effect that is often used to enhance the sound of an electric piano (see pages 144–145). A chorus and some other popular effects are demonstrated in Tipcode Piano-017.

Recording

If the module has a built-in digital *sequencer* or *recorder*, you can record your playing. This is a very helpful feature:

- You can record the right-hand part of a piece, play it back, and **then play the left-hand part along to it.**

- You can play back what you have just recorded simply to hear what you sounded like and **evaluate your performance.**

- You can record **ideas for compositions**, rather than writing them down.

- The sequencer can also be used to play a **four-handed piece on your own**, and so on.

Events

Sequencers do not record sound, but they digitally record the 'events' of your performance: the keys you press, the velocity at which you do so, the release of the keys, the effects you use, the pedals you press, and so on.

Memory

The capacity of a sequencer is usually expressed as the number of events it can hold in memory, and sometimes as the number of notes. A '1,600-note song memory' may sound impressive at first, but at a moderate tempo you play that many notes in a matter of minutes. For sound modules a capacity of 30,000 is not unusual.

Memory full

If the sequencer's memory is full, you need to delete one or more recordings, or you should be able to store them on an external hard disk or your computer. For this purpose, the sound module needs to feature a USB port or another type of connection.

103

Line out

Many sound modules have special outputs (*line out* or *audio out*) to connect the module to a stereo system or another external amplifier, so you can also listen to your music — live or recorded — without headphones.

Audio in

An input for sound signals (marked *line in* or *audio in*) can be used to hook up a CD player or another audio source to the piano. This allows you to play along with other recordings without disturbing anyone.

Operation

Some sound modules have all the controls on the box itself; others have the most important controls to the left of the keyboard or elsewhere closer at hand. These may be easier to reach, but they're also more visible.

Polyphony

Often, brochures will say something about the number of notes that the sound module can produce at the same time. If the module offers *16-voice polyphony*, it can play sixteen notes at once. That sounds like a lot — you only have ten fingers — but in fact you'll often need more. After all, if you sustain a chord and carry on playing other notes, you soon use more than ten sounds or voices simultaneously. A 64-voice or 64-*note* polyphony will typically be sufficient, but some instruments (e.g., professional digital pianos) offer 128-note polyphony.

Expanded possibilities

Most sound modules allow you to expand the possibilities of your piano in another way too. You can now hook it up to a computer, a synthesizer, or any other electronic instrument.

Computer

If you connect your piano to a computer, you can have the computer print out what you play in notes, you can record your performance (including strings, brass, percussion, and any other instrument) and edit it later, or you can use the computer as a teacher — all provided your computer has the software and the hardware to do so.

Piano keys, synthesizer sounds

If you link a synthesizer to your sound module, you can produce the sounds of that synthesizer by playing the keys of your piano. You can turn it around too, playing the sounds from your module using the synth's keyboard.

MIDI

All this is made possible by a system called MIDI. This stands for *Musical Instrument Digital Interface*. Basically, MIDI translates the notes you play (and their loudness and other data) into standardized codes. These codes can be 'read' and converted to sound by any type of device that uses MIDI.

MIDI out

The simplest sound modules only have a MIDI output. This allows you to control other instruments from your piano, or to record your performance on your computer, for example

MIDI in

A MIDI input allows you to send MIDI data to your sound module. This allows you to control its sounds from another keyboard, for instance, or you can use your module to play back what you recorded on your computer.

MIDI thru

A third type of connector is MIDI thru, which allows you to include the instrument in a daisy-chain of MIDI equipment.

Five-pin connectors or USB

Traditionally, MIDI uses round five-pin connectors. A growing number of manufacturers use a USB-type port instead.

More information

There's more about sequencers and MIDI in *Tipbook Keyboard And Digital Piano.*

105

PLAYER PIANOS

Player pianos are pianos that play by themselves. Basically, they're not very different from silent pianos. What sets them apart is that player pianos have a jack under the very end of every key. These jacks (*solenoids*) are controlled by the sound module, which activates the keys, thus replacing the pianist's fingers.

Record...
The idea is very simple. A pianist plays a piece on an instrument with built-in sensors that register all the key and pedal movements very precisely. This performance is recorded digitally.

... and reproduce
Afterwards, the process is reversed. The player system converts the digital recording to signals that 'tell' the jacks exactly which keys to play and how hard. The pedals can be controlled in much the same way. The result is a modern player piano: a piano that plays itself. These systems don't come cheap; they can cost as much as five to twenty thousand dollars.

Famous pianists
Player pianos can be used to record and reproduce your own playing, but you can also bring famous pianists into your living room, as a recording stored on CD, or other media. On a real instrument they'll always sound better than on even the best hi-fi system. Or you can let a master pianist play the right-hand part, while you play the left-hand part yourself. Most new computer techniques and storage systems are quickly finding their way into these types of systems.

Brands
Well-known player piano systems include ConcertMaster (Baldwin), Disklavier (Yamaha), PianoDisc, Pianoforce, and QRS/Pianomation. Pianodisc can be combined with video, a 20" flat

screen on the music desk displaying anything from silent movies to slide shows, lyrics, and chord symbols. Pianoforce was the first to allow you to control their system with an iPhone or iPod touch.

DIGITAL PIANOS

As an alternative or in addition to an acoustic piano, you can get a digital piano. Some digital pianos look very much like the real thing; others, so-called *stage pianos*, look more like a home keyboard or a synthesizer.

A stage piano.

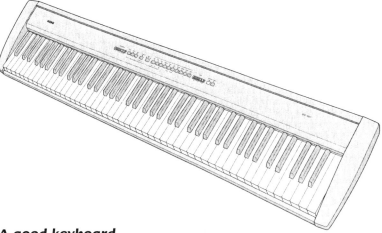

A good keyboard
To make good digital pianos feel like their acoustic counterparts, small hammers are often built into their actions, their only function being to provide the desired feel. These keyboards come with names such as *hammer action*, *hammered action*, and *weighted action*. Some digital grands even have a genuine grand piano action.

Touch-sensitive
Of course, a digital piano has to be *touch-sensitive*: The sound gets louder if you play harder — and not only louder, but a little brighter too, just like an acoustic piano.

107

A basic digital piano with a weighted action.

Not quite the same sound

However good a digital piano is, it will never sound the same as an acoustic piano. One of the main reasons is that the sound comes from a set of speakers, rather than being produced by a soundboard.

No strings

Digital pianos also sound different because they don't have strings, and non-existent strings can't 'sing' along, for instance when you

The future

As time goes by, digital pianos will get closer and closer to the acoustic instrument. When this book went to print, the latest generation of digital pianos allowed for tuning the instrument per string (rather than per note), for example. In many respects, these instruments even tend to surpass their ancestor, featuring the possibility to adjust the resonance or the voicing of the instrument on the spot, adjusting the sound to the style of music you want to play, or to the room acoustics.

press the sustain pedal. That said, a growing number of digital instrument emulate this string resonance effect for a more natural, acoustic sound.

Learning to play

Even then, most teachers feel that you will learn to play better on a good acoustic piano than on a digital one. The difference between acoustic and digital instruments gets bigger the better your technique gets. An acoustic instrument allows you to color the sound by the way you play the keys; digital instruments don't — yet.

Options

Most digital pianos have more options than the sound modules usually installed in acoustic pianos: more sounds, more effects, a more powerful sequencer (more tracks, a larger memory, editing facilities, etc.), and so on. MIDI and other inputs and outputs are standard features.

The price

Digital pianos cost less than acoustic ones. A good-sounding digital piano with a piano-like action will set you back some less than a thousand dollars. For some three to seven thousand dollars you can get yourself the very best, with numerous sounds and all the options you could wish for. On the other hand, digital instruments don't last as long as acoustic pianos, and they lose their value a lot sooner. Then again, digital instruments need no maintenance and don't have to be tuned, voiced, or regulated.

More information

For more information on digital pianos and their possibilities, please refer to *Tipbook Keyboard And Digital Piano.*

8

Accessories

An introduction to some of the main accessories for piano players: piano benches and stools, piano lamps, and caster cups. The chapter ends with a brief section on piano amplification.

Most pianists prefer rectangular benches rather than the smaller, round seat of a stool. Benches and stools are both available in hard-top and upholstered or padded versions. Hard-top seats can be made more comfortable with separately available bench pads. The most luxurious benches, often featuring a diamond tuffed vinyl or even leather upholstery, are known as artist benches. *Tip:* Benches may provide you with sheet music storage under the seat.

Upholstery
If you decide to go for a padded version, then note that a leather upholstery is very luxurious, but vinyl is easier to clean. A fabric upholstery is less sticky and sweaty than vinyl. A selection of colors is available, with black being the most popular choice.

Height-adjustable
Playing is easier and less tiring if you sit at the right height. It also reduces the risk of back and neck aches. Not all benches are height-adjustable; most stools are. Usually, the difference between the highest and the lowest position is some three to six inches. Some seats can be adjusted as low as 16" or as high as 25".

Non-adjustable
Non-adjustable benches are available in different heights, to match either the player or the instrument. *Grand benches* may be about an inch lower than *upright benches*, as the keys of a grand piano are a bit lower than those of an upright. Grand benches are often a little wider too.

Knobs or a spring
So-called artist benches have two large knobs to adjust the height. Others systems use a spring. If various people used the chair and the height needs to frequently adjusted, a bench or chair with a gas spring, gas lift or gas shock — similar to the ones used in office chairs — may be the best choice.

Spinning the seat
Stools are typically height-adjusted by spinning the seat. Usually this means that you'll have to re-adjust the height from time to time, as the seat also spins a little when you stand up or sit down.

Some stools have been designed to prevent that from happening. Expect to pay around a hundred and fifty dollars or more for a good stool that won't wobble after years of use.

> ### Chairs
> *Some players prefer a traditional piano chair, which has the added comfort of a back rest. Piano chairs are available in adjustable and non-adjustable versions. Some chairs have shorter front legs, so the seat slopes toward the piano.*

TIP

Legs
To make a bench perfectly match your piano and your interior, you can choose from a variety of leg styles, ranging from Queen Anne and Louis XV to square-tapered or brass ferrule variations, and many more.

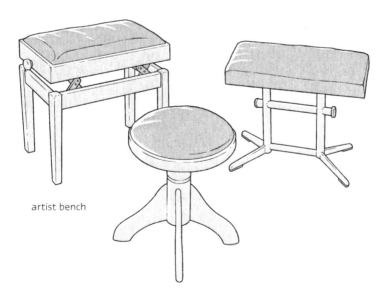

artist bench

Developments
Next to the traditional type of benches and stools described above, various companies make special ergonomically designed chairs with seat gradient adjustment, a vertically and horizontally adjustable back rest, special padding, and other features.

113

More expensive

A good bench will easily cost you two to three hundred dollars, but there are adjustable benches for as little as a hundred dollars. Extra money may buy you extra sturdiness, a longer lifespan, or just a more exclusive design. Some people take exclusivity to extremes, and there are benches that sell for over two thousand dollars. Other specialties include *duet benches* on which you can adjust the height of both seats separately, or benches with a seat that can be tilted.

LAMPS

Most piano lamps are fairly classical, brass designs, but others have a more modern look. Both types come with either halogen lamps or traditional light bulbs. For grand pianos, there are special versions that you can clamp to the music desk. If the lamp needs to stand on the back part of an upright's lid, because the front part is open for playing, then a model with a boom arm can be handy.

All kinds of models...

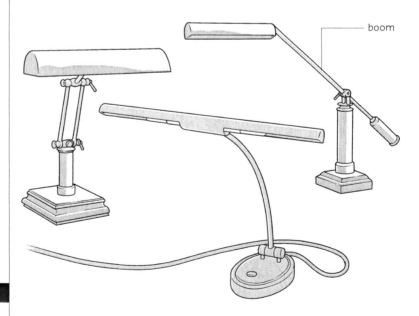

boom

Piano lamps easily cost one to four hundred dollars. One of the main differences between a piano lamp and an ordinary one is that the first usually has two light sources so that it can light the entire keyboard.

CASTER CUPS

Casters, small ones especially, tend to leave deep marks in most types of carpet. The solution is a set of caster cups. Of course, the cups should be removed when you want to use the casters to move the piano.

All kinds of materials
Caster cups are available in all kinds of materials (wood, plastic, glass) and finishes (satin or high-gloss; walnut, ebony, mahogany, etc.) to match the instrument or the floor. Prices range from about twenty to more than fifty dollars for a set of three cups.

... in various materials and heights...

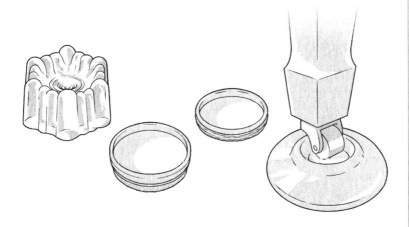

Reduce the sound
Caster cups may help reducing the sound a piano transmits to the floor, and there are special caster cups that have been designed for that purpose.

115

Too low

If the keyboard of a piano sits very low — or if you are very tall, or both — the whole instrument can be placed onto extra high caster cups. A tip: The higher the caster cups are, the harder it will be to comfortably reach the pedals.

MICROPHONES AND PICKUPS

Should you need to amplify a piano, or if you want to record an acoustic piano, it's good to know that there are dedicated microphone systems for (grand) pianos available. Brand names include EarthWorks, AMT, and Audix. As an alternative, you can use one or two (condenser) microphones that can be positioned over or inside the open top, above both the treble and the bass strings, or some eight inches from the bass and treble sides of the soundboard, for example. The position of the microphone(s) strongly influences the sound (natural, full or thin, tubby or bright, amount of hammer attack, etc.) as well as the risk of feedback and leakage from other instruments. The latter two problems can be countered by using pickups or transducers instead.

Pickups

Transducers or *pickups* literally 'pick up' the vibrations of the soundboard and convert them to electric signals, which are sent to the amplifier. Similar pickups are used on acoustic guitars, violins, and other acoustic instruments. Usually, one pickup won't be capable to truly capture the entire range of a piano, so it's better to use two of them. Positioning the pickups, again, is of major influence on the resulting sound. Dedicated piano pickups are made by companies such as Barcus Berry, Blue Star Music, Helpinstill, K&K, Schatten Design, Schertler, and Yamahiko.

116

9

Maintenance

A piano requires less daily maintenance than most other instruments. All you really need to do is to keep it clean and make sure that the relative humidity and temperature in your home don't cause problems.

When it comes to piano maintenance, there are many things you'd best leave to professionals. This includes moving the instrument, tuning, voicing, regulating, and even some of the cleaning. Chapter 10 tells you all about these subjects.

High-gloss or satin

To free high-gloss or satin finish from dust, simply use a soft, lint-free cloth. Swiffers and similar dusters may work fine too; please check that they don't scratch. Wipe in long, straight lines rather than in circles, and exert as little pressure as possible: Strange as it may sound, dust can scratch. You may begin by using a very slightly damp cloth, to pick up the dust. Most fresh fingerprints can be removed by first breathing on them, so that the lacquer mists over. *Tip:* High-gloss finishes, especially black, tend to show every speck of dust on the instrument's surface.

French-polished instruments

On French-polished pianos or instruments treated with wax, a soft, dry cloth will usually do, provided the instrument is cleaned regularly. If it needs more work, ask an expert.

Cleaners

Special cleaners are available for every type of finish, typically costing some ten to fifteen dollars a bottle. That doesn't sound cheap, but you may only use it once a year, so it'll last a long time. The instructions that come with the cleaner tell you which finishes it is suitable for. Some piano cleaners have an anti-static (i.e., dust repellent) effect.

Household cleaners

Don't use household cleaners on pianos. They're often too abrasive, and they may leave a residue or even damage the finish. Always avoid using silicone based cleaners, as they may damage the action.

Soap

To remove marks on high-gloss and satin lacquer finishes, you may moisten a soft cloth with a mild soap solution (e.g., a mild cleaning liquid or shampoo).

Polishing polyester
Those very fine scratches that can quickly show up in polyester finishes can be removed with special polishing agents. If you want to stay on the safe side, let your technician take care of this. Before using any kind of polishing liquid, always dust off the instrument. Deeper scratches or dents can be filled. For invisible repairs please consult a professional.

Wax
If you have a piano finished with wax, or an older satin-finish instrument, you can treat it very lightly with beeswax once a year. Experts advise against using a wax that contains silicones. Never use wax on pianos with a synthetic outer ply (see pages 44–45).

French polish
French-polished instruments require special care, so please consult a specialist.

Keys
Clean the keys with a dry or slightly damp cloth, moving from the back to the front of the keys rather than sideways. If the keys are plastic-covered, you may spray a very small amount of glass cleaner onto the cloth — not onto the keys themselves — or use a

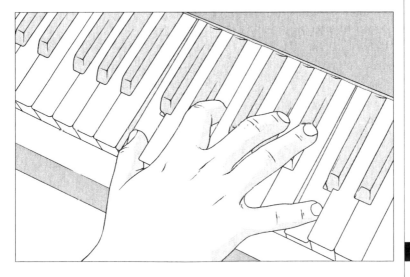

The sides of the keys get dirty too.

119

special key cleaner. Always dry the keys immediately after cleaning them. The color of ebonized black keys can sometimes rub off. If so, don't use the same cloth to clean the white keys.

The sides
Now and again, clean the sides of the keys too, as they get dirty when you play the neighboring keys.

> ### Ivory
> *Don't use glass cleaners or other cleaners on ivory-covered keys, and dry them off at once: Ivory is sensitive to moisture. Another tip: Make sure the cloth you're using will not stain the keys.*

The inside?
The inside of the piano is best left to your piano technician. If you want to clean it yourself, please limit yourself to using a vacuum cleaner to get rid of the dust that gathers at the bottom of an upright. Take off the lower panel, which is usually held in place by a simple clamp. Don't touch the strings or any parts of the action and the pedal work with any part of the vacuum cleaner, and always use a soft, long-haired brush attachment.

Grand piano
Dust under the frame of a grand piano is very hard to get rid of, so better leave this to a technician too. Never use a hair dryer to blow the dust away: The heat may damage the soundboard, and the dust will usually settle somewhere else in the instrument, making the problem only worse.

Moths
The anti-moth treatment the felt receives in the factory eventually vanishes. Keeping the instrument dust-free helps to keep moths away. If moths are already a problem or you think they might be, you may install odor-free moth paper on the inside of the upper frame. Technicians can do this for you too.

Woodworm
Playing your instrument helps prevent woodworm, as these animals apparently don't like vibrations. If the wood shows lots of tiny holes, call an expert.

Questions
When you buy an instrument in a store, you will often be told what maintenance is required. You can also ask your technician if you have any questions: List them on pages 214–215.

PREVENTION

You can avoid a lot of cleaning, polishing, and repairs by these tips.

Keep it closed
Close the lid and the fallboard when you are not playing. This prevents dust from settling in the action and the windings of the bass strings. Wood-finished instruments may discolor unevenly if the fallboard is always open: The wood will keep its original color only where the fallboard rests against the upper panel. Direct sunlight, which should be avoided at all times, will speed up any discoloration.

Clean hands
Washing your hands before playing helps keeping the keys clean. Handling the fallboard and lids by the bottom edge or sides as much as possible helps to avoid visible fingerprints on the instrument.

No flowers, plants, or drinks
Don't put flowers or plants on the piano. The action is sensitive to moisture, and the finish may be as well. (French-polish is very vulnerable!). For the same reason, don't put drinks on the cabinet or on the *key blocks* or *end blocks* (the small flat areas at either end of the keyboard).

121

Scratches

If you do put photo frames, lamps, or anything else on the instrument, make sure there's felt underneath. Even music books scratch most finishes, eventually.

Candles

Spilled candle-wax is difficult to remove without damaging the finish, and it's especially annoying if it ends up between the keys. Keep candles away from the instrument.

> ### Strings and felt
> Avoid touching the strings or felt parts because your natural skin oil and the acids it contains are not good for them: Felt gets greasy and strings rust.

Cover

If the instrument is used in a public place, consider protecting it with a cover. They are available for both grand pianos and uprights, completely covering the instrument.

Moving

At some time you may want to shift your piano within your house or apartment. If you are in any doubt, leave this to professional piano movers (see page 128), especially if you are planning to move it to another room. This will help prevent damage to your instrument, your house, and yourself.

DRY AND MOIST, HOT AND COLD

In many houses, the relative humidity (RH) and temperature are so steady that a piano can happily grow old there. But if conditions are really dry or humid, if the humidity changes fast and often, or if the room temperature in the room is very low for some time, you can get all kinds of problems. The soundboard can crack, panels can warp, keys can stick and tuning pins come loose, and so on. Fortunately, all of these developments are preventable.

Dry

If it's freezing outside and the heating is on indoors, the air gets drier and drier, with most heating systems. As your lips chap, wood will contract. If the soundboard contracts, the crown (page 76) gets lower, which reduces the tension on the strings. *Tip:* Air conditioning systems also make the RH-level drop.

Moist

In summer, the air is at its most moist. In humid conditions, wood expands. That means the tension on the soundboard increases, and with it the tension on the strings. As a result, the pitch will go up. If it gets really humid, keys can stick, just like doors, drawers and windows. All kinds of other parts of your precious instrument can suffer from moisture: Damp hammer heads produce a squidgy sound, the action may get (and stay) noticeably heavier, strings can rust, and ivory key covers can come loose. Old houses with gas heaters are usually quite damp.

Forty to sixty

Many experts say the best humidity level for pianos — and for people — is between 40% and 60%. It won't matter if the relative humidity briefly goes outside of that range, but if it lasts any longer you may have problems.

Changes

It's at least as important that the humidity doesn't change too fast. You should take that into account if you move an instrument from an old house with gas heat to a much drier apartment with central heating and air conditioning, or the other way around.

Hygrometer

You can measure humidity using a *hygrometer*, on sale from all piano stores. The most affordable models, costing around twenty dollars, have a dial and a pointer. Digital hygrometers are more expensive, but they're usually more accurate and often include a thermometer.

123

Calibrating

There is another difference. A dial-type hygrometer, which uses a hair to measure the humidity level, gets sluggish and becomes steadily less responsive. However, if you leave it outside for a night, the moist air will refresh it for a whole year. Better still, you can recalibrate it yourself. Around the time of year when the weather gets colder and you switch the heating back on, wrap it in a wet cloth for a quarter of an hour and immediately afterwards set the pointer to 98%.

A digital hygrometer and a traditional hair hygrometer.

Sunlight and heating

Wood heats up and dries out if you leave it too close to a heater, and putting a piano above a heating vent is asking for trouble.

Temperature

Pianos are like people when it comes to temperature as well. Around 65–70°F (18–21°C) is typically best. Temperatures lower than 60°F (16°C) may cause problems, so it's advisable to keep the heating on in the winter, even if you're not there. The more steady the temperature and humidity, the more stable the tuning of the instrument will be.

124

Direct sunlight is just as bad, certainly if it shines straight onto the soundboard of the instrument. Finishes can be easily damaged by direct sunlight too.

Extra measures

Whether you need to take extra measures to keep the humidity at the right level depends on a lot of things. For instance, houseplants and an open kitchen cause extra moisture in the air, whereas a very well-stocked bookcase helps to keep the humidity a little more constant. To keep things constant, an upright piano is better off standing near an inner wall than a thin outer wall.

Too dry?

Really, the biggest problem is excessively dry air. Be careful when temperatures drop below 32°F (0°C). Some people try to keep humidity up to the required level by sticking a rolled-up newspaper into a container half-full of water and standing it in the bottom of an upright piano. The newspaper helps the water to evaporate, but this will take a long while. What's more, it may go moldy, the moisture may cause rust, and the whole thing could fall over or, more likely still, simply be forgotten. So don't!

Internal climate control

As an alternative, there are internal climate control systems that keep the humidity level inside the instrument at a stable level (42%, according to Technical Bulletin #3 of the Piano Technicians Guild; see page 172). Advanced systems can counter both high and low humidity levels. If the air is too dry, the built-in hygrostat automatically switches on the moisturizer; if the air is too damp, a drying unit is activated. A warning light comes on when you need to refill the tank. Including installation, such systems usually cost around three to six hundred dollars. Damp-Chaser is the best-known brand name.

Other systems

There are many other internal systems, ranging from very basic and affordable water-filled tubes to more advanced humidifiers, hygrostats, and heating elements. Check out their prices and the maintenance they require.

The whole room

There are also various types of devices that humidify the entire room, rather than just the instrument. This extends the benefits of a better climate to you and your furniture, for instance. Each system has its own advantages and drawbacks. Some of the more common systems are listed below.

Hot and cold systems

Steam humidifiers are available from around seventy-five or a hundred dollars. They work fast and generate some extra heat, which some people find much too damp. What's more, you can hear some models bubbling away when they're switched on. Cold humidifier systems are quieter, but more expensive. They take longer to work, and they need quite a lot of maintenance (cleaning, filling, and so on); some systems require additives for the water. Some are also capable of drying the air during humid periods. Depending on how your house is heated, it may also be a good idea to have a central humidifier installed.

Look and compare

A few tips: Visit a few different stores and ask about these and other systems, compare prices and power consumption, ask whether you need any extras and what they cost, and consider the maximum volume of air each device can handle. Larger rooms may need two. Humidifiers are available from stores that sell household appliances as well as from piano stores.

10

Transportation, Tuning, and Regulation

A pianos typically needs to be tuned two or three times a year. If you want to keep it in prime playing condition and extend its life span, it also needs to be regulated every few years. New strings, new hammers, and many other new parts can be fitted in due time, if required. All of those jobs are best left to professionals, and the same goes for moving the instrument.

Moving a piano is best left to an established firm of piano movers. If you are buying from a store, delivery is usually included in the price; if you are buying from a private owner or if you're renting the instrument, it usually isn't.

Costs
The costs of moving a piano vary between roughly a hundred and four hundred dollars, excluding a mileage charge. The exact price may also depend on the size and the value of the instrument. Other additional charges may be for stairs (per number), the need to use a crane, or anything else that makes the job harder.

TIP

Binding quote
Always ask for a binding quote in advance — but you will only get one when the movers know exactly what the job involves.

Indoors
Even if a piano only has to be moved from one room to another, it's a good idea to call a professional company.

Specialized
Specialized piano movers can be found online or through piano stores. *Tip:* Check if the movers are insured for any damage they may cause.

Space
Check beforehand whether the instrument will fit where you want to take it, and don't forget to look at the dimensions of doors or windows, staircases, and other relevant obstacles. Some movers may even come and take a look themselves.

Damage
If you're going to move a pre-owned instrument, always check it for any scratches and other damage. Include the former owner in this check-up. This helps to avoid disputes about damage being caused during transportation.

128

TUNING

A guitar or a violin has to be tuned every time it is played. A piano doesn't. Two or three times a year is often enough. A new instrument may need one or two extra tunings the first year or two.

Out of tune

Every piano goes out of tune eventually, even if it hasn't been played. One reason is that the tension of the strings varies with changes in humidity and temperature (see page 122 and onwards). The more stable those two factors are, the more stable the tuning of the instrument will be. Tuning stability depends on the instrument itself too: Better pianos often detune less than low-budget instruments.

Piano tuners and technicians

Tuning a piano is a job for a professional, from the 'setting' of the tuning pins to the precise tuning of over two hundred strings to

Tuning a piano requires an expert.

each other. Many piano tuners are also piano technicians, so they do repairs and adjustments too.

Certified technicians
Every country has one or more organizations of certified piano tuners and technicians, where you can apply for member addresses (see pages 172–173 for details). Ask other piano owners whether they know a good tuner or technician, or let a piano salesperson advise you.

How much
A normal tuning soon takes an hour to an hour and a half. The price typically varies from seventy five to a hundred and fifty dollars, depending on where you live, the proficiency or the reputation of the tuner, and other factors.

How often
If you play about five to ten hours a week, it's usually enough to have your instrument tuned two to three times a year. If an instrument needs to be tuned more often or if it goes out of tune very quickly, something is wrong with it, or with the conditions in the room, or with the tuner / technician: One thing that sets good tuners aside is that they provide the instrument with a stable tuning.

When
As changes in temperature and relative humidity can strongly affect the piano's tuning, it's usually considered best to have your piano tuned in the spring and in the fall.

More often
New and recently re-strung instruments need to be tuned more often, one reason being that new strings will stretch before they stabilize. Some tuners, technicians, and piano makers will state that one extra tuning per year for the first few years is enough, others prefer to give a piano two extra tunings in the first year. The particular instrument plays a role in the decision too.

Too late

If you can clearly hear that a piano is out of tune, you're really too late in getting it tuned. The more a tuner / technician has to adjust it, the harder it is to produce a stable tuning. What's more, more turning of the tuning pins causes more wear to the pinblock.

TIP

Pitch drops

Some pianos never seem to go out of tune. Should you still have them tuned regularly? Yes, because they do go out of tune, but it happens so slowly that you may get used to it — which doesn't help developing a good ear for pitches. If a piano is not being tuned, the pitch will drop over the years, the bass section usually a little less than the other octaves.

Too low

Some pianos may still sound in tune, even if the pitch has dropped. Then too, tuning is necessary. A piano that sounds too low can't be used with other instruments (unless you can tune them down to the piano), and it won't sound as good as it can: Pianos are designed to sound their best at A=440 (see page 85). And of course, the further the tuning has dropped, the harder it will be to bring the instrument back to the right pitch, even with a *double tuning* or *pitch raise* (i.e., raising the tension of the strings to their average correct levels before fine tuning the instrument).

Just moved

If a piano has just been moved, it often needs to get used to its new environment for two or three weeks. There's a fair chance that it will suddenly go out of tune or not play as well in that time. Don't call a piano technician until those few weeks have passed. Only then are tuning and regulating useful. Also, those few weeks may allow you to discover that the instrument needs additional voicing to adjust its sound to the acoustics of the room.

Electronic tuner?

There are electronic tuning devices for pianos, but they don't replace a technician. Technicians may use one as an aid, but it'll never replace their ears. Also, there are books that promise to teach you to tune your piano yourself — but no book can substitute the knowledge and experience of a good technician.

EQUAL TEMPERAMENT

A piano is difficult to tune because it has so many strings, but that's not all. The following section explains some of the backgrounds of piano tuning, and it tells you why two tuners will always tune an instrument slightly differently. If you want to avoid a little bit of musical math, you may skip ahead to page 134.

Twice as fast
The A that most instruments are tuned to, can be found slightly to the right of the center of a piano keyboard (A4) At that pitch, the strings vibrate at a speed of 440 vibrations per second (440 hertz). Eight white keys or an octave higher, at A5, the strings vibrate twice as fast (880 hertz).

One and a half
Likewise, there are specific ratios for all other intervals. For example, if you go up a fifth (five white keys, e.g., C4 to G4), the strings at that key will vibrate one and a half times as fast.

Problem
Now, there is a slight problem — one that experts have wrestled with for centuries. In the illustration on the opposite page you'll see what's wrong: The different ratios don't match. The calculation shown above the keyboard fixes the note A5 at a different pitch (880Hz) from the one shown below the keyboard (891Hz).

Hiding
The solution? Tuners and technicians 'hide' these discrepancies by tuning most of the notes a tiny bit too high or too low. These discrepancies are so minute that you may need a trained ear to hear them. For instance, C4 is tuned to around 262 hertz, rather than 264.

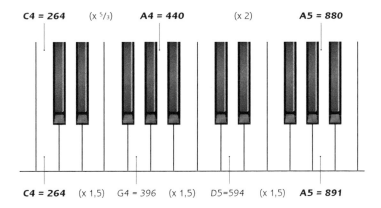

C4 = 264   (x ⁵/₃)   **A4 = 440**   (x 2)   **A5 = 880**

C4 = 264   (x 1,5)   G4 = 396   (x 1,5)   D5=594   (x 1,5)   **A5 = 891**

The solution

Tuners and technicians have to decide how much they allow certain notes to deviate. They do so by listening to the 'beats' that various combinations of two notes produce.

Beats

If you play C4 and G4 together on a properly tuned piano, and listen carefully, the sound seems to vibrate a little. You can actually count the vibrations or *beats* that these two pitches produce when played simultaneously. Faster beats can be heard when you play C4 and A4 together. These beats betray the fact that even a well-tuned piano is slightly 'out of tune'. If it were perfectly tuned, you wouldn't hear any beats.

Equal temperament

On a piano, nearly every combination of two notes will produce beats, however slightly. In other words: The discrepancies (the mathematical errors, so to speak) are equally spread across the whole keyboard. This is known as *equal temperament* or the *well-tempered* scale.

Differently in tune

By listening very closely to these beats, the tuner knows how much too low or too high each note needs to be tuned. Exactly which frequencies he chooses to achieve a balanced tuning depends on the individual tuner. That means that a different tuner or technician may make your piano sound just slightly different. Of

133

course, you may prefer one tuning — and thus, one tuner — to another.

Meantone tuning

It is possible to tune a piano perfectly and without hearing any beats. Such a *meantone tuning*, as used before equal temperament was introduced, has its limitations, however: With meantone tuning, an instrument can sound in tune in just a few keys only. If you tune it so C-major sounds perfect, it will be terribly out of tune B-major, F-minor, and other keys. Equal temperament offers the solution. It makes it possible to tune a piano so that it can be used in all key signatures.

TIPCODE

Tipcode PIANO-018
A meantone tuning in C makes the B and A-flat major scales sound terribly out of tune.

REGULATING AND VOICING

The more you play and the older the instrument is, the more servicing it will usually require. On the other hand, your piano will need less frequent maintenance if you keep the lid and fallboard closed when you are not playing it; your technician does some minor maintenance and checks the regulation and voicing as well as the tuning; or if you play for only a few hours a week. The quality and the condition of the instrument also play a role. A good technician will help you keep an eye on all of those things. If something goes wrong in the meantime, from breaking strings to sticking keys or creaking pedals, call an expert at once.

Regulating

Every instrument needs to be regulated periodically. This means adjusting the action and the pedals and everything that's connected to them, so the piano plays the way it should, providing a uniform response along the entire keyboard, control over the tone and the dynamics, and allowing you to play anything you want.

Voicing

Over the years, the felt of the hammer heads gets denser and harder, which makes the tone steadily thinner and edgier. That's why every instrument needs to be voiced sooner or later (see also page 66). Hammers can be reshaped if they have become flattened, or if the strings have worn deep grooves into them, provided there is still enough felt left and it is in good condition. Hammers can be softened by inserting *voicing needles*, or they can be hardened in different ways. Rather than improving a piano's performance, voicing can also be required to adjust the tone of the instrument to your liking or to the room's acoustics.

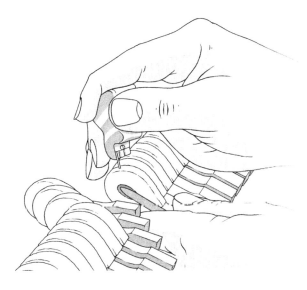

Making hammer heads softer by pricking them.

Reconditioning

As the parts of the piano are exposed to wear, temperature and humidity changes, and aging, there will come a time that tuning, regulating, and voicing aren't sufficient any more to make your instrument sound good and play well. By that time, major servicing, generally indicated as *reconditioning*, is necessary. What exactly needs to be done depends on the age and the condition of the instrument, among other things.

Rebuilding

If major parts (strings, pinblock, action, etc.) have to be replaced, technicians speak of (partially) *rebuilding* the instrument, which will be as good as new, or even better. Of course, the instrument should be worth the cost of such an operation.

11

History

The action in today's grand pianos is not that much
different from the one Bartolomeo Cristofori built some
three hundred years ago. Even so, there have been
plenty of developments since his day — and of course,
much went on before too.

As early as the fourteenth century, and perhaps even before, there was an instrument with keys and strings: the *clavichord* (*clavis* means key, *chord* means string). When played, small brass wedges made the strings vibrate very softly.

Plucking

The harpsichord, which was most popular in the seventeenth and eighteenth centuries, sounded a lot bigger and fuller than the clavichord. Harpsichord strings were originally plucked by the quills of raven feathers that were attached to the ends of the keys.

Spinet and virginal

A *spinet* works like a harpsichord, but it is a size smaller, and the strings run at an angle backwards from the keys. On a *virginal*, another variant, the strings usually run perpendicular to the keys, from left to right.

The oldest preserved piano, a Cristofori, built in 1720, with a range of four-and-a-half octaves, no pedals, and two-string unisons for each note.

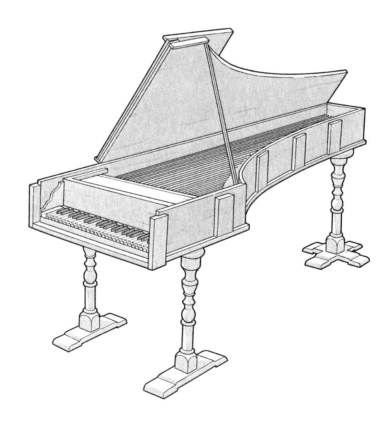

Touch-sensitive

Harpsichords, spinets, and virginals are not touch-sensitive. Every note sounds equally loud, no matter how the keys are struck. This was a problem the Italian harpsichord maker Bartolomeo Cristofori (1655-1731) set out to solve. Around 1700 he began building an instrument that would be able to sound both loud and soft, based on the harpsichord but using hammers instead of raven quills.

Piano e forte

The result, which he unveiled a few years later, he christened the *gravicembalo col piano e forte*, literally meaning 'harpsichord with loud and soft.' A good quarter of a century after his first experiments, Cristofori came up with an improved action, which was very similar to the present system.

Pianoforte, fortepiano

The full name of the instrument was soon shortened to *pianoforte* or *fortepiano*. Just like harpsichords and spinets, these forerunners of the modern piano are still used to play the music of that era. The main difference is that the tone of a pianoforte or *hammerklavier*, produced by leather-clad hammers, is often described as more transparent, brighter, and shorter than that of a modern grand piano.

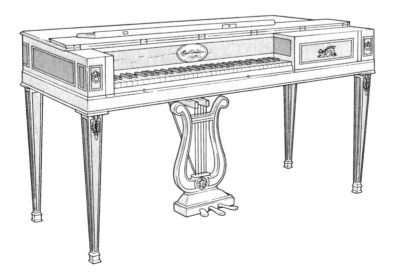

A square piano with over five octaves and a lyre with three pedals (Pleyel, 1816).

139

Square piano
From about 1750 to 1850, the *square piano* or *square grand* was very popular. Its horizontal strings ran from left to right through a rectangular cabinet.

Vertical
The first upright pianos were built midway through the eighteenth century. Names like *giraffe piano* and *pyramid piano* indicate that such instruments came in all kinds of shapes and sizes. The precursor of the modern upright piano appeared around 1800. Matthias Müller, Isaac Hawkins, and Robert Wornum are the three names most often mentioned in its development.

Inventions
Since Cristofori, a whole lot of things have been changed, invented, and improved. For instance, in 1821 the Frenchman Sébastien Érard devised the *double escapement* mechanism or *repetition mechanism*, the system that allows the greater repetition speed of a grand piano. Before that, Érard had already introduced the agraffes and other innovations.

Pape
Érard's compatriot Henri Pape was also responsible for countless inventions and improvements, from introducing felt (rather than leather) hammer heads to the cross-strung upright piano. Steinway, a manufacturer with more than a hundred patents,

TIP

Louder
Larger concert halls meant that pianos had to produce more volume and a bigger sound, so ever-heavier gauge strings were introduced over the years. In turn, those strings needed bigger hammer heads to set them in motion, and the increased string tension required a cast-iron frame, which the American piano maker Alpheus Babcock patented in 1825. The soundboard also became steadily thicker, and the number of octaves grew from four and a half to more than seven.

140

produced the first cross-strung grands midway through the nineteenth century.

Player piano

A very different invention, dating back to the end of the nineteenth century, is the *player piano*. This instruments works much like a barrel organ, which has paper rolls punched with holes that tell the mechanism which notes to play. These days, player pianos use digital technology (see Chapter 7).

An English piano built around 1800 (Robert Knight, London).

A hundred years

Little has changed in the last hundred years or so, but of course piano makers have not been idle. The results of their efforts range from using synthetic components to player grands with built-in

141

CD players, and from various systems to make uprights repeat faster, to special cabinet designs, and to smaller-sized keyboards to fit children's hands.

Only a few

Then there are lots of other models of which only a few are ever built. Plexiglas grands, for example, or pianos with a glass soundboard, instruments with eight extra keys per octave so that you can play quarter-tones too, or double grands with two keyboards and two soundboards, or instruments for left-handed pianists, with the bass notes on the right (see page 160)! For the youngest aspiring pianists, even four octave mini grands are available.

12

The Family

Pianos are referred to as string instruments, but also as percussion instruments, because the strings are struck by hammers — and they're known as keyboard instruments too. This chapter introduces you to some of the relatives of that part of the family.

Basically, pianos belong to the family of string instruments, like guitars and violins. Within that family they fall under the category of keyboard instruments, as do the harpsichord, the spinet, and the fortepiano mentioned in the previous chapter. In this chapter you'll find descriptions of some other keyboard instruments. The digital piano, which appeared in the early 1980s, is covered in Chapter 7.

Hammered dulcimer

The only family member without keys in this chapter is the *hammered dulcimer*. The strings of this instrument are sounded by striking them with hammers, just like a piano's. The difference is that you hold the hammers yourself. You are most likely to see the dulcimer, also known as *cymbalo* or *cymbalom*, in gypsy orchestras.

Celesta

A *celesta* or *celeste* looks like a small piano but is actually a glockenspiel with keys; the hammers strike metal plates that produce a ringing tone. The sound is very soft, and the instrument is scarcely used outside of classical music.

Accordions

The *accordion* is a keyboard instrument too. The left hand plays bass notes and chords on a *button keyboard*, featuring up to 120 small, round buttons. The right hand, playing the melody, has either a standard keyboard layout or a button keyboard or *chromatic keyboard*. When you stretch or squeeze the bellows of the instrument, the air flow makes one or more metal reeds vibrate, just like in a mouth organ or mouth harp.

Electric piano

The *electric piano* is a forerunner of the digital piano. Instead of strings, most electric pianos use metal forks, tongues, or tines that are struck by hammers. The vibrations are picked up by one or more magnetic pickups (like on an electric guitar), and from there are sent to the amplifier. Some of the main electric piano names include the Fender Rhodes, the Wurlitzer, and the Hohner Clavinet. Many digital pianos and piano modules feature samples of these sounds.

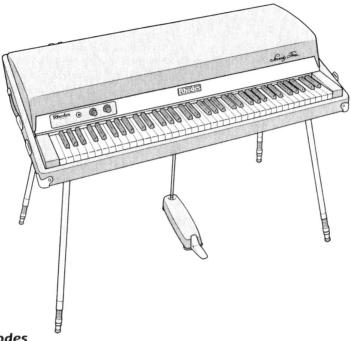

Fender Rhodes
Stage Piano.

Rhodes

The arrival of digital pianos made electric pianos disappear eventually, but a respectable number of musicians continued playing their old Rhodes pianos. In 2008, the new Rhodes company introduced a new edition of the instrument, which now features MIDI.

Organ

An organ may look like a piano, but it is actually a very different instrument, which is played very differently too. One major difference is that where a piano note decays after a while, an organ will sound until you let go of the key. This is just one reason why organs require a different playing technique. On classical or church organs, air is blown through a large number of flute-like pipes. Using various combinations of pipes per key, organs can produce different timbres. Contrary to pianos, organs are not touch-sensitive; most of them have a volume pedal.

Tonewheel organ

Tonewheel organs use a notched, rotating 2" disc for each note and

145

a magnetic pickup for each disc. The notches produce changes in the magnetic field of the pickups, similar to what the vibrating strings of an electric guitar do. The number of notches (two for the lowest note, 256 for the highest note) determines the pitch.

Hammond B3

The best-known tonewheel organ is the Hammond B-3, made from 1954 to 1974. Even though it has been digitally emulated, with designs that duplicate the original instrument at a fraction of its 400-pound weight, the vintage B-3 is still preferred over these newer models by many rock and jazz musicians.

Hammond B-3 tone wheel organ.

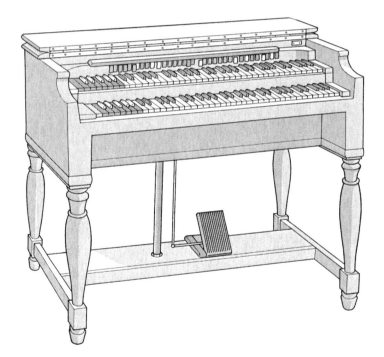

Home keyboard

Home keyboards were developed from the organ. Apart from a number of organ sounds, home keyboards offer have dozens or hundreds of other sampled sounds, from guitars and strings to drum sets, clarinets, rain showers, gunshots, and helicopters. Keyboards come with a standard automatic accompaniment

146

feature: Play a chord, choose a tempo, and the built- in virtual band starts playing — so all you have to do is play the melody or a solo.

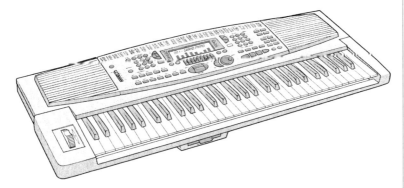

Hundreds of sounds, automatic accompaniment, built-in amplification, and much more.

Piano?

Most home keyboards also offer a choice of piano sounds. Even so, you can't really 'play the piano' on this instrument, for one thing because most home keyboards don't have a weighted action (see page 107).

Synthesizer

To synthesize means to produce or combine artificially. With a synthesizer you can make your own sounds. The instrument usually has a number of basic sounds that you can edit in all kinds of ways — digitally, acoustically, or both — to create new sounds. There are software synths too, which allow you to use your computer as a musical instrument.

More and more alike

The differences between instruments like synthesizers, keyboards, and digital pianos are getting ever smaller. You can buy digital pianos with home keyboard options, there are home keyboards with synthesizer options, and synthesizers with weighted keys. *Tipbook Keyboard and Digital Piano* takes a closer look at all of those digital instruments.

147

13

How They're Made

Some piano factories build their instruments one by one; others have mass production lines. Some factories produce thirty pianos per year, others thirty thousand, or even more. Of course, there are many other differences between one factory and the next. Generally speaking, though, pianos are built in the way described below.

Building a piano takes time to do properly. A high-end instrument can easily take more than two years to craft, from the moment the first planks are sawn to the final tuning and voicing. The wood used for expensive instruments has often been dried and cured for five to ten years.

TIPCODE

Tipcode PIANO-019
This Tipcode takes you on a guided tour in a piano factory.

Soundboard

Most soundboards are made of solid spruce planks about four inches (10 cm) wide. The ribs are glued at right angles to the grain of the soundboard. A press may be used to create the crown, among other techniques. On the other side of the soundboard are the bridges over which the strings will run.

Frame

The frame is made in a special foundry, and then filed, sanded smooth, drilled, and finished. The holes for the two-hundred-plus tuning pins must be drilled in exactly the right places.

Strings

Like the frame, the steel strings are almost always purchased from an outside supplier. The only part of string manufacture that piano factories often do themselves is the winding of the bass strings.

First tuning

Once the pinblock is in place, the strings are stretched over the soundboard and tuned for the first time. Since there are no hammers yet, the tuner plucks the strings as a guitarist would. This process is called *chipping*. After tuning, the entire structure — consisting of the frame with back posts, soundboard, strings, and pinblock — is given time to settle. The strings, now under tension, are able to stretch until they reach a fairly stable length.

The cabinet

Meanwhile, in a different part of the factory, the cabinet is being manufactured. Curved wooden parts, like some fallboards or the rim of a grand piano, are usually bent into shape using large presses or numerous clamps.

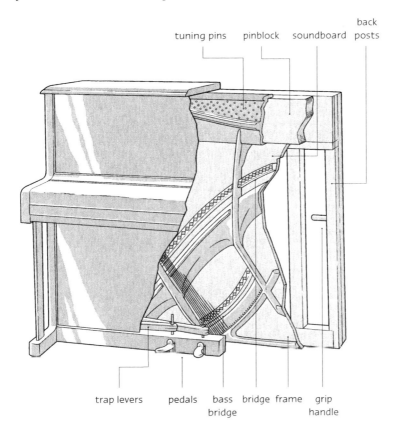

tuning pins   pinblock   soundboard   back posts

trap levers   pedals   bass bridge   bridge   frame   grip handle

The cabinet, the back posts, and the rest.

Finishing

Finishing the wooden case usually involves many steps, including staining, filling, sanding, and polishing.

151

Sawing the keyboard

The keyboard is sawn from a large piece of laminated wood, somewhat like a giant jigsaw puzzle. The sharps — small black plastic or wooden bars — are glued on afterwards.

... like a giant jigsaw puzzle...

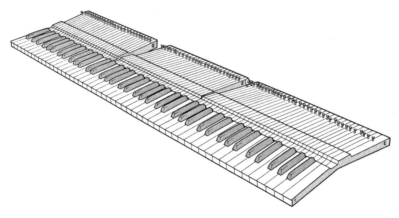

Installed

Once the frame, soundboard, and strings have been installed in the cabinet, the action, the keyboard, and the pedals are fitted.

Regulation

The regulation of the instrument takes a lot of time, if done properly. For example, all the keys must be perfectly balanced, so weights are used to determine how much lead, if any, needs to be added to each key. In addition, each key must be exactly level with all the others, and the key dip should be the same for every key. All the dampers must respond equally quickly. And so must all the hammers, all the let-off buttons, all the pilots, all the repetition springs, all the whippen-top flanges, and all other parts.

Voicing and tuning

Proper voicing is a time-consuming business too, mainly consisting of giving the hammers the desired hardness by inserting needles in the felt. Often instruments will be voiced more than once, just as they are tuned and regulated several times. Higher-quality instruments are often broken in by machines that play them for many hours before they leave the factory.

14

Brands

There are hundreds of piano brands, with names old and new: Famous names, obscure names, family names and made-up names. This chapter offers a short introduction to the main piano brands and makers, and sheds some light on a very complex market.

In the first half of the twentieth century there were many, many piano factories in the USA and Europe — hundreds of them, mostly rather small, each with its own brand name. Today, only a few of those companies still exist. Most have vanished, and a few ever-larger factories, mainly in Asia, build instruments under a wide variety of brand names, often using the names of those old companies. According to the Blue Book of Pianos, there are 'some 12,000 piano brand names catalogued worldwide' (www. bluebookofpianos.com/pianos.html)!

One makes, many brands

One Asian piano manufacturer may make pianos under a dozen or more different brand names, next to producing instruments under their own trade name. Conversely, there are piano brands that have been made in at least four different factories within a twenty-year time span.

Confusing

This is just a minor indication of how complex the piano market is. You can buy a piano with a reputable brand name today, and find out that the name was actually sold to a not-so-reputable piano maker not long before. Buying your instrument at a trustworthy dealer is the best way to make sure you buy a good instrument, backed by a proper warranty. The following is merely an indication of the brands you may come across, and it's by no means intended to be complete.

Germany

The piano is an Italian invention, and many of the first improvements came from France and England. Even so, German manufacturers soon built up the most impressive reputation — and many companies all over the world advertise their use of German parts for their instruments, from Kluge keyboards to Abel hammer heads. German pianos do not come cheap, often starting around seven or eight thousand dollars.

Names

The image that German pianos have explains why German-sounding names are often used on pianos, just like Asian-built steel-string guitars often have American names. Names of famous composers are also very popular, so you may come across pianos under the names of Schubert, Strauss, Schumann, or Wagner, for example. These brand names, of course, don't tell you anything about the actual quality of the instrument.

Countries

Knowing the country an instrument comes from may be of little help too. For instance, you can buy Chinese pianos with European parts, but European pianos with Chinese parts are just as common. Also, there are 'Japanese' pianos that are completely assembled in Europe or America (like cars), and American companies that have part or all of their instruments made in Asia.

Image, price, and quality

A country's reputation for building pianos is often reflected by the prices charged for those instruments. Germany has a great reputation. Of course they do, you'd say: The Germans make higher quality – and thus higher priced – instruments only. Other countries, where less expensive instruments are made, typically have or used to have a less favorable reputation. The bottom line of this story? The quality of an instrument is not necessarily related to its origins, but rather to its price. Expensive pianos are usually better instruments than low-budget ones — so there's not much of a difference with any other type of product. That said, you may very well come across a lower-priced piano that sounds better than its more expensive neighbor!

House and stencil brands

There are many more makes than the ones listed on the following pages. Among them are also a large number of so-called private labels, house brands or stencil brands. Piano stores, importers, and distributors can simply order a number of pianos and have their own brand name put on them.

• If the instruments have certain features consciously chosen by the dealer, they're usually referred to as a **house brand**.

• If they are a standard model, only the brand name being different, they're typically called **stencil pianos**.

Time sensitive

Most of the information in this chapter is quite time sensitive. While most major brands are likely to be around for many years to come, other brands may be discontinued; also, companies may decide to have their instruments build in another country, or brand names can be bought by another company, not necessarily producing instruments of similar quality. Check dedicated websites, piano magazines, and other sources for up to date information (see pages 170–173).

Unlisted brands

The fact that a brand name is not listed in this chapter does not say anything about the quality of the pianos. There are simply too many brands available to include them all.

The brands

The following section starts with brief descriptions of some of the traditional and/or larger names in the piano industry. A variety of other companies, some larger, some even older, are listed starting on page 159.

BECHSTEIN

Bechstein (1853) is the best know and oldest brandname of the German Bechstein Gruppe, which also includes the German-made **C. Bechstein**, **Bechstein Academy** and **Zimmerman** brands, as well as the Czech-made **W. Hoffman** and **Bohemia** brands, **Euterpe** (Indonesia) and **Wilh. Steinmann** (China).

KAWAI

Kawai (1927), one of Japan's largest piano makers, has instruments made in Japan and Indonesia. **Shigeru Kawai** is their top line of instruments. **Boston**, a Steinway sub-brand, is made by Kawai. The company also makes digital pianos.

The world's largest piano maker, the Pearl River Piano Group of Guangzhou, China, makes Pearl River as well as **Ritmüller** pianos, and provides private label brand pianos internationally. In addition, the company produces a line of stringed instruments. Ritmüller was one of the first German piano makers.

PETROF

Petrof (1864), the Czech brand made in Europe's largest piano factory, produces uprights and grands in virtually all sizes. **Scholze** and **Rösler** are part of the Petrof group. Petrof also makes parts for other piano manufacturers.

Samick®

One of the biggest companies in the music industry, Samick (Korea) makes pianos and guitars in Korea, Indonesia, and other countries, under their own trade names (e.g., **Pramberger**, **Wm. Knabe**, **Kohler** and **Campbell**) as well as for many other companies. Wm. Knabe instruments are designed, developed, assembled and finished in the US.

SAUTER®

Besides their conventional models, the German company Sauter (1819) makes various modern uprights in striking designs with matching benches.

SCHIMMEL®

Schimmel (1885) is one of the largest European manufacturers. As well as building classic models, this German firm has always been a leading innovator.

157

Eduard Seiler started his company in 1849, and like quite a few other German brands, the company has been run by the descendants of the founder for many generations. Schimmel's **Vogel** pianos are made in Poland.

The one-man organ factory started by Torakusu Yamaha in 1889 is now one of the world's largest builders of musical instruments, mostly under their own name. The Japanese company also makes a large variety of other products, from motorbikes to hi-fi equipment. Yamaha's **Cable Nelson** pianos are made in China.

YOUNG CHANG

Young Chang (Korea) is one of the many Asian companies in which German experts play an important role. Instruments are being made in South Korea and China. **Weber** pianos come from this company too, and Young Chang owns Kurzweil, maker of digital keyboard instruments.

High-end instruments
A few companies are exclusively known for their high-end instruments: Bösendorfer (Austria), Steinway, and Fazioli (Italy).

Bösendorfer

Bösendorfer was founded in 1828 in Vienna, where the factory is still located. One of the most exceptional instruments of the company is a 97 key grand. The nine extra bass keys turn this Model 290 Imperial into an eight octave instrument.

STEINWAY & SONS.

Steinway has two factories, one in Hamburg, Germany (the original home of the family, then called Steinweg) and one in America, where Steinway & Sons was founded in 1853.

Fazioli

The Italian **Fazioli** company, makes the world's longest grand piano, the F 308 (10'2"), featuring a fourth pedal, the unique pianississimo pedal.

Made in the US

Only a very limited number of companies still produce (mostly high-end) pianos in the US. **Steinway** is the best known name. **Mason & Hamlin**, located in Boston since 1854, produces 350 high-end instruments per year: 50 uprights, and 300 grand pianos. **The Walter Piano Company** was founded by Charles R. Walter, who introduced his first Charles R. Walter piano in 1975. Most **Baldwin** pianos are made in China; some high-end grand pianos are still US made. **Fandrich & Sons** doesn't make pianos, but they build their Fandrich Vertical Action in Asian-made uprights.

(Former) US brands

Many brands that used to be made in the US now come from Asian factories. Some examples are **Hallet, Davis & Co** (Dongbei), **Kohler & Campbell** (Samick), **Krakauer, Everett, Falcone** and **George Steck** (Sejung), **Weber** (Young Chang), **Story and Clark**, and **Wm. Knabe and Knabe**.

North-American brands made overseas

Not all Chinese made pianos come from Chinese owned companies. **Baldwin**, for example, is owned by guitar maker Gibson. A few high-end Baldwins are still being made in the US; all other pianos come from China. **Wyman**, a relatively young brand founded by former Baldwin employees, is another example of an American owned company making pianos overseas. **Heintzman** pianos were made in Canada until the early 1980s; today's instruments come from China.

China: European names

China has become one of the main piano making countries. The exact number of piano manufacturers is unknown, but there are at least a hundred of them. Next to the makers of Pearl River (see page 157) some of the better known names include the Beijing Hsinghai Piano Group (**Otto Meister**, Wyman, and others), the Dongbei Piano Company (owned by Baldwin, making Baldwin

159

and **Nordiska** pianos, and brands listed elsewhere in this chapter) the Shanghai Piano Company, and Yantai-Perzina (**Perzina, Carl Ebel**, **Gerh. Steinberg**). Perzina, a Dutch-owned company, distinguishes itself by featuring a floating soundboard. Nordiska was a Swedish company; Perzina (1871), Carl Ebel (1877), and Gerhard Steinberg (1908) were founded in Germany.

China: new names

Not all Chinese-built pianos come under European names, and not all these pianos are low-budget instruments. One example would be Palatino (2000), a company that also makes stringed instruments. Some of the many other original Chinese brand names include Hailun, Milton, and Trianon.

Cars and pianos

Just like Yamaha makes both motorbikes and pianos (and much more), the Korean name Hyundai can be found on both cars and pianos. Likewise, you may come across Suzuki and Daewoo cars (now Chevrolet) and pianos.

Germany

There are numerous other German brands besides the names listed above. Some better-known examples:

- **Blüthner**, featuring aliquot strings in the high treble of its grand pianos. The company also makes mid-priced instruments under the Haessler name; Irmler and Breitman are Blüthner trade names as well. A Blüthner specialty is a small range of left-handed pianos, made to order.

- **Grotrian** (1835), another company that focuses on the higher price range, has been family-owned for five generations;

- **Ibach** (1794) is the oldest surviving piano company. At one time, it had instruments made in Korea;

- From the start of the 21st century, **Förster** pianos are exclusively German-made pianos. Before that time, the name was also used for instruments made by Petrof (see page 157);

- **Pfeiffer** also supplies **Hupfeld** and **Rönisch** instruments;

- **Feurich** is run by Julius Feurich, of the fifth generation of this piano making family;

- **Wilh. Steinberg**, a medium-sized factory that, among its other models, produces the most affordable German-built upright ;

- **Steingraeber** (1852) is one of the few companies where you can have your instrument custom made.

- **Brückner** and **Steinmann** also come from Germany.

Britain
One of the best-known British piano makers is **Kemble**, established in 1911. Whelpdale, founded in 1876 as an importer for Blüthner, supplies the smaller brands **Knight**, **Bentley**, **Welmar**, **Marshal & Rose**, and **Broadwood**, among others. **Woodchester**, established in the former Bentley factory, was founded in 1994 and discontinued before this book went to print.

Poland
Th. Betting used to be one of the most famous Polish brand names. Theodor Betting, founder of the company, also established the Polish piano company **Schirmer & Son**. Other brands with Polish origins include **Calisia** (since 1878; originally using the Fibinger name), **Ravenstein**, and **Steinbeck**.

Czech Republic
In addition to the larger companies described above, the Czech Republic houses some smaller piano brands too. One example would be **Seidl**.

Other countries

- **Estonia** pianos, named after their native country, are made by the original Tallinn Piano Factory (1893).

- **Pleyel** was founded in 1807 by the French composer Ignace Pleyel. The same company also made Gaveau, Rameau, and Érard pianos. Schulmann was a lower-budget Asian-made Pleyel brand.

161

- The **Furstein** and **Schulze-Pollman** brand names sound German, but the instruments are made in Italy.

- **Fritz Dobbert** pianos (1950) are made in Brazil.

More information on these and other piano makers can be found online and in some of the books listed on pages 170–171.

Glossary

This glossary briefly explains all the jargon touched on so far. It also contains some terms that haven't been mentioned yet, but which you may come across in other books, in magazines, or online. Most terms are explained in more detail as they are introduced in this book. Please consult the index on pages 216–218.

Acoustic piano
The qualification 'acoustic' only became necessary after electric and (later) digital pianos had been introduced. In other words, an acoustic piano is a regular piano, i.e., a piano that can be played without the use of an amplifier.

Action
The mechanism that makes you play the instrument, consisting of dozens of wooden, felt, leather and metal parts per key. The smallest upright pianos have an *indirect blow action* or *drop action*, which is mounted below the keys. Taller pianos have a *direct blow action*.

Agraffes
Brass string-guides.

Baby grand
A small grand piano.

Bach pedal
See: *Pedals.*

Back posts
Wooden posts, reinforcing the structure of an upright piano. The posts in a grand piano are called *braces.*

Bass
The lowest notes, produced by copper-wound strings.

Belly
See: *Crown.*

Bird-cage action
See: *Overdamper.*

Braces
See: *Back posts.*

Bridge
The bass and treble bridges transmit the vibrations of the strings to the soundboard.

Caster cups
Placed under a piano's casters to protect the floor, and sometimes to reduce sound transmission.

Casters
Piano wheels are called *casters.*

Celeste pedal
See: *Practice pedal.*

Concert grand
The tallest grand piano.

Console
Small type of upright. See: *Spinet.*

Covered strings
See: *Wound strings.*

Cross-strung pianos
By allowing the strings to run diagonally, so that the bass strings cross the other strings, longer strings can fit inside an equally large cabinet. Also called *over-strung pianos.* Early pianos were *straight-strung.*

Crown
The arch or *belly* of the soundboard.

Dampers
Felt dampers mute the strings when you let go the keys.

Digital piano
A piano without strings; the sounds are samples (digital recordings).

Direct blow action
See: *Action.*

Down weight
The force needed to play a soft note. See also: *Up weight.*

Duplex scale
A system that includes the far end of the higher treble strings in the sound production.

Escapement
See: *Let-off.*

Equal temperament
Equal temperament tuning (a.k.a. *well-tempered scale*) allows pianos to be played in all key signatures.

Frame
The cast-iron frame that, together with the back posts or braces, forms the backbone of an upright or grand piano. Also called the *plate.*

French polish
Old-fashioned, expensive finish for pianos. The material used is *shellac.*

Front lid
The front part of a grand piano lid.

Hammer heads, hammers
Piano strings are struck with felt hammers.

Hybrid piano
An acoustic piano with a built-in digital piano module. See also: *Silent piano.*

Indirect blow action
See: *Action.*

Keyboard
Pianos usually have eighty-eight keys, although some older keyboards have eighty-five. See also: *Keys.*

Keys
The keyboard usually has fifty-two ivory or synthetic-covered white keys (naturals) and thirty-six synthetic or wood black keys (sharps).

Let-off
The let-off makes the hammer go back after hitting the string. Also known as *escapement* or *set-off.*

MIDI
Using MIDI, you can hook up all kinds of electronic musical equipment (digital pianos, sound modules, synthesizers, and so on) to each other, or to computers.

Moderator stop
See: *Practice pedal.*

Music desk
Pianos always have a built-in music desk.

Mute pedal
See: *Practice pedal.*

Naturals
The white keys. The black keys are known as *sharps.*

Octave
An octave is an interval that spans eight white keys (i.e., from one C to the next). A piano keyboard has a good seven octaves.

Overdamper
Some (very) old uprights have the dampers above the hammers. Also *called bird-cage action.*

Over-strung
See: *Cross-strung.*

Pedals
Pianos have two or three pedals. The *sustain(ing)* or *damper pedal,* on the right, removes all the dampers from

the strings. The left-hand pedal of an upright is the *soft pedal*; on a grand it's called the *una-corda pedal*, reducing and altering the sound by slightly shifting the hammers. The middle pedal is usually a *practice pedal* or *mute pedal* on uprights, activating a muffler, and a *sostenuto pedal* on grands. A sostenuto pedal makes only those notes already played sustain; it's also known as *Steinway pedal* or *Bach pedal*.

Pinblock
The tuning pins are set into a hard-wood pinblock. Also called *wrest plank*.

Plate
See: *Frame*.

Player piano
A piano that plays itself. The modern version works digitally, and can be used for recording too.

Practice pedal
On uprights, the middle pedal is often used to lower a strip of felt between the hammers and the strings, muffling the overall volume for practicing purposes. The same system (also known as *celeste*, *moderator stop*, *muffler pedal* or *mute pedal*) is available in hand-operated versions as well.

Pressure bar
Strings are held in place either by a *pressure bar* or by *agraffes*. See also: *Agraffes*.

Regulating
The action of a piano needs periodic regulation in order to make the instrument play well and sound good.

Rim
The 'cabinet' of a grand piano.

Scale
Everything connected with the choice of strings is collectively called the scale, from the number of strings to their thickness, their length, their winding, and much more. Many instruments feature a German scale.

School piano
A piano with protective brackets, large wheels, and extra locks

Set-off
See: *Let-off*.

Sharps
The black keys. The white keys are known as *naturals*.

Shellac
See: *French polish*.

Silent piano, silent system
A piano with a silent system allows you to practice in silence. A stop rail prevents the hammers from hitting the strings, while the keys you play trigger the digitally recorded (piano) sounds from the instrument's sound module. Silent pianos are also known as hybrid pianos.

Solid wood
Most soundboards are made of planks of solid spruce. Other parts (pin blocks, for instance) are virtually always laminated, made up of several plies of wood.

Sound module
A box containing digital recordings (*samples*) of a piano or other instruments.

Soundboard
The soul of a piano. The soundboard amplifies the sound of the strings.

Speaking length
The part of the string that vibrates, producing a note, when struck with a hammer. See also *Duplex scale.*

Spinet
1. Spinet piano. The very smallest upright piano (up to some 40" or 100 cm high).
2. A historical keyboard instrument with plucked strings.

Steinway pedal
See: *Pedals.*

Straight–strung
See: *Cross- strung.*

Strings
A piano has around two hundred and twenty steel strings. Only the lowest bass notes have one string each. The upper bass notes have two strings each: These are the double or two-string *unisons*. From the first low treble notes upwards there are three strings per note (i.e., three-string unisons).

Studio piano
Medium to full-size upright piano.

Sustain pedal, Sustaining pedal
See: *Pedals.*

Tenor
See: *Treble.*

Treble
The highest five octaves (approximately) of a piano, sometimes divided into *low treble* or *tenor* and *high treble*, the latter referring to the highest three octaves.

Tuning pins
Steel pins used to tune the strings. Also called *wrest pins.*

Una-corda pedal
See: *Pedals*

Unison
See: *Strings.*

Up weight
The force with which a key comes back up.

Vertical piano
Another name for upright piano.

Voicing
Treating the hammer heads to adjust or improve the tone of the instrument.

Well-tempered scale
See: *Equal temperament.*

Wheels
See: *Casters.*

Wound strings
The bass strings are wound with copper wire, the extra mass allowing them to sound low enough without becoming too long. Likewise, the lower pitched strings on guitars and stringed instruments are wound strings.

Wrest pins
See: *Tuning pins.*

Wrest plank
See: *Pinblock.*

167

Tipcode List

The Tipcodes in this book offer easy access to short videos, sound files, and other additional information at www.tipbook.com. For your convenience, the Tipcodes in this Tipbook have been listed below.

Tipcode	Topic	Chapter	Page
PIANO-001	Various styles of music	1	**2**
PIANO-002	An octave; eight white keys	2	**6**
PIANO-003	Practice pedal	2, 3, 5	**8, 24, 80**
PIANO-004	Upright action	2	**11**
PIANO-005	Grand action	2	**16**
PIANO-006	Una-corda pedal	2, 5	**16**
PIANO-007	Sostenuto pedal	2,5	**17, 83**
PIANO-008	The range of a piano	2	**18**
PIANO-009	Let-off or escapement	5	**59**
PIANO-010	Dampers; no dampers	5	**65**
PIANO-011	Sustain pedal	5	**78**
PIANO-012	Hybrid piano's mute rail	5, 7	**81, 100**
PIANO-013	Tuning fork	5	**86**
PIANO-014	Three test chords	6	**93**
PIANO-015	One test chord	6	**93**
PIANO-016	Various sounds	7	**102**
PIANO-017	Effects	7	**102**
PIANO-018	Meantone tuning & equal temperament	10	**134**
PIANO-019	Inside a piano factory	13	**150**

Want to Know More?

Tipbooks supply you with basic information on the instrument of your choice, and everything that comes with it. Of course there's a lot more to be found on all of the subjects you came across on these pages. This section offers a selection of magazines, books, helpful websites, and more.

MAGAZINES

The following magazines are of interest for most pianists:

- *Pianist*: www.pianistmagazine.com

- *International Piano* (UK): www.pianomagazine.com

- *Piano Today*: www.pianotoday.com

- *The Piano Technicians Journal*: www.ptg.org

- *Clavier Companion*: www.keyboardcompanion.com

BOOKS

There are dozens of books on pianos, ranging from publications on the history and workings of the instrument to photo books and extensive descriptions of the way they are built. The following is a limited selection.

- *The Piano Book – Buying & Owing a New or Used Piano*, Larry Fine (Brookside Press, 2001, fourth edition; 244 pages; ISBN 978-1929145010; also available in hardcover). An annual supplement describes all changes in the piano market and lists prices for every brand and model of new piano on the market (over 2,500 of them), plus advice on how to estimate actual selling prices (see www.pianobook.com for more information).

- *Piano – Evolution, Design and Performance*, David Crombie (Barnes & Nobles, 2000; 112 pages; ISBN 978-0760720264).

- *The Complete Idiot's Guide to Buying a Piano*, Marty C. Flinn and Jennifer B. Flin (Alpha, 2008; 336 pages; ISBN 978-1592577187)

- *Piano Servicing, Tuning and Rebuilding, For the Professional, the Student, the Hobbyist*, Arthur A. Reblitz (Vestal Press Ltd., 1996; 327 pages; ISBN 978-1879511033).

- *The Cambridge Companion to the Piano*, Davis Rowland (Cambridge University Press, 1998; 260 pages; ISBN 978-0521479868).

- *Piano Roles – A New History of the Piano*, James Parakilas (Yale University Press, 2002; 320 pages; ISBN 978-0300093063).

- *Piano Roles – Three Hundred Years of Life with the Piano*, James

Parakilas (Yale University Press, 2000; 461 pages; ASIN B000X6G3MA).

• *Giraffes, Black Dragons, and Other Pianos: A Technological History* from Cristofori to the Modern Concert Grand, Edwin M. Good (Stanford University Press, 2001; 400 pages; ISBN 978-0804745499).

• *The Piano: An Inspirational Guide to the Piano and Its Place in History*, John-Paul Williams (Billboard Books, 2002; 160 pages; ISBN 978-0823081516).

• *The Piano* (The New Grove Series), Philip Belt (W.W. Norton Company, 1998; 190 pages; ISBN 978-0393305180).

• *The E Book of Pianos; price guide for pianos.* Available online (www.bluebookofpianos.com).

Additionaly, the Piano Technicians Guild has published a number of Technical Bulletins with worthwhile information on finish care, humidity control, and related subjects. These are of interest for all piano owners. Ask you registered piano technician (RPT).

INTERNET
Internet addresses tend to change fast, but with a bit of luck some of the following sites will give you a good starting point and countless links to other sites. You may also find a teacher or a tuner / technician via these sites or the others mentioned elsewhere in this section.

• The Piano Education Page: pianoeducation.org

• The Piano Home Page: www.marthabeth.com/piano.html

• The Piano Page (Piano Technicians Guild): www.ptg.org

• The UK Piano Page (Association of Blind Piano Tuners: www.uk-piano.org

• Piano World: www.pianoworld.com

• The Blue Book Of Pianos: www.bluebookofpianos.com

• www.americanpianists.org

171

LOOKING FOR A TEACHER?

If you want to find a teacher online, try searching for 'piano teacher' and the name of area or city where you live, or visit one of the following special interest websites:

- PrivateLessons.com: www.privatelessons.com

- MusicStaff.com: www.musicstaff.com

- The Music Teachers List: www.teachlist.com

- www.pianoteachers.com

- pianoeducation.org/pnotchrl.html

- The Virtual Piano Shop: www.americanpianists.org

PIANO TECHNICIANS AND TUNERS

You can find a certified piano technician through the following organizations:

USA and Canada

- Piano Technicians Guild (PTG): www.ptg.org

- Piano Technicians Guild, Canadian chapters: www. canadianpianopage.com

- Master Piano Technicians of America: www. masterpianotechnicians.org

- Canadian Association of Piano Technicians (CAPT): www. capianotechs.ca

- Ontario Guild of Piano Technicians: www.ogpt.ca

Australasia

- Australia and New Zealand: Australasian Piano Tuners and Technicians Association (APTTA): www.aptta.org.au

UK

- Piano Tuners Association: www.pianotuner.org.uk

- Association of Blind Piano Tuners: www.uk-piano.org

Other countries

For other countries, additional information and updated details, please check the website of the Piano Technicians Guild (see above).

Chords

One of the great things about the piano is that it allows you to play chords. To fully and musically use that enormous potential, and to increase your understanding of the music you're playing, it's good to have some basic knowledge of the subject.

Songbooks, books featuring jazz or rock standards, and most songs that you can download from the internet come with chord symbols that tell you which chords to play to the music. It may take you some time to learn how to translate some of these symbols to the actual notes that you should play. If so, the numerous chords depicted on pages 190–213 will help you out. Both basic and advanced chords are included.

Traditional notation

Classical music doesn't use chord symbols. Instead, the notes that make up chords are simply printed on the staff. This traditional notation can be found in many songbooks also.

Broken chords

If you play classical music, you will often play so called *broken chords*: Instead of playing the three or more notes that make up a chord all at once, you play them one after the other, as shown in the left-hand part of the music below. The first two bars show four (broken) C major chords. This chord is made up of the notes C, E, and G. In the next two bars, you play an inverted G7 chord with an omitted fifth. What this all means will be explained on the next couple of pages.

A few bars from a sonatine by Anton Diabelli (1781–1858).

Play around

So if you're a classical player, the music will simply tell you which notes to play, without explicitly demanding that you know which chords you're actually playing. Still, it's good to know a little more about chords. Why? Because it helps improve your understanding of the music you're playing, which may make you a better player. Also, it may help prevent mistakes as you not only know that you should play a B♭ rather than a B in a certain chord, but you know why, too. The many chords presented in this section may inspire you to try them out and play around with them, increasing your understanding of the subject.

Improvisation

If the music you play invites you to play solos, the notes of the chords offer you a safe starting point for your improvisation. For an advanced level of playing, you should of course also know the scales that those chords are based on. This goes beyond the scope of this section, so scales are not included here.

Chords per root note

Chords are names after their root note: There are all kinds of C chords, C♯ chords, and so on. This section presents chords by their root note, with a double page for each note. You will find all C chords on pages 190–191, all D♭ chords on the following two pages, etc. Every left-hand page shows three and four note chords; five note chords are shown on the right-hand pages.

Four groups

The chords are presented in four main groups:

- Major chords: chords with a major third (3).

- Minor chords: chords with a minor third (♭3).

- Dominant chords: chords with a major third (3) and a minor seventh (♭7)

- Diminished chords: chords with a minor third (♭3) and a diminished fifth (♭5).

Variations

Each main group of chords includes a number of variations, such as major chords with lowered or raised pitches (e.g., ♭5 or ♯5).

Accidentals per chord

Note that all chords on pages 190-213 have their own accidentals, e.g. a flat (♭) or a sharp (♯) in the first chord is valid for that specific chord only, and not for any of the following chords on that same staff.

TIP

Chord symbols

Most chords can be indicated with various chord symbols. On the chord pages of this section, only the most common symbols have been used. Most other chord symbols can be found in the table on pages 180–183, which also lists the construction of the various types of chords and their full names.

Steps

The table also shows the *steps* or *scale degrees* of each type of chord. For example, a major chord is made up of the degrees 1–3–5: the root note (1, also indicated as R), a major third (3) and a perfect fifth (5). These scale degrees are also used throughout the text on the following pages. In most cases, the text also includes an example of the chord in actual pitches, using C chords most of the time.

Intervals

To take full advantage of this section of the book, you should have a fair knowledge of basic music theory, including the intervals and accidentals (sharps and flats). If you don't, please check out *Tipbook Music On Paper* (see page 222).

Chord diagrams

All chords in this book are shown in traditional music notation. Alternatively, chords can be displayed as chord diagrams, indicating the keys that should be played. An example is shown below. Please check out Tipbook Keyboard and Digital Piano for such diagrams (see page 221)!

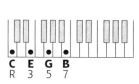

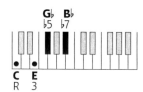

CHORD CONSTRUCTION

So how are chords constructed? The basic principle is quite straightforward. Here's the C major chord.

- The root note is the first note (1) of a chord. In C major that's a C.

- The second pitch sounds a major third (3) higher. In C major that's an E.

- The third pitch sounds a perfect fifth (5) higher than the root note. In C major that's a G.

Major
So the C major chord consists of the pitches C–E–G. Just like any other major chord, its steps are 1–3–5 or R–3–5.

Minor
In a minor chord, the second pitch is a minor third, so C minor has the pitches C–E♭–G. All minor chords have the following construction: R–♭3–5. The flat (♭) lowers the third a half step.

Augmented
An augmented chord is made up of two major thirds: R–3–♯5. The sharp (♯) raises the fifth a half step. C augmented consists of the notes C–E–G♯.

Four
All chords mentioned so far consist of three pitches. There are also chords with four or more pitches. Those extra notes, known as extensions, are typically indicated by adding numbers (steps) to the chord symbol. *(Continued on page 182)*

TIP

Stacked thirds
Chords basically consist of stacked thirds. A major chord consists of two of these intervals: a major third (1-3) and a minor third (3-5). In a minor chord, the order of these thirds is inverted: 1-♭3 is a minor third, and ♭3-5 is a major third. A diminished chord has two minor thirds — and so on.

179

Chord symbol	Alternative symbols	Pitches (C)
Major		
C	–	C, E, G
Csus4	–	C, F, G
C2	–	C, D, E, G
Csus2	–	C, D, G
C6	–	C, E, G, A
Cmaj7	CΔ	C, E, G, B
C6/9	–	C, E, G, A, D
Cmaj7^9	CΔ^9	C, E, G, B, D
C$\flat$5	–	C, E, G$\flat$
Caug	C+	C, E, G$\sharp$
C$\sharp$4	–	C, E, F$\sharp$, G
Cmaj7$^{\sharp5}$	C$\Delta^{\sharp5}$	C, E, G$\sharp$, B
Cmaj7$^{\flat5}$	C$\Delta^{\flat5}$	C, E, G$\flat$, B
Cmaj7$^{\sharp11}$	C$\Delta^{\sharp11}$	C, E, G, B, F$\sharp$
Cmaj7$^{9\,\sharp11}$	C$\Delta^{9\,\sharp11}$	C, E, G, B, D, F$\sharp$
Cmaj7$^{\flat6}$	C$\Delta^{\flat6}$	C, E, G, A$\flat$, B
Cmaj7$^{9\,\flat6}$	C$\Delta^{9\,\flat6}$	C, E, G, A$\flat$, B, D
Cmaj7$^{9\,13}$	C$\Delta^{9\,13}$	C, E, G, B, D, A
Cmaj7$^{9\,\sharp11\,13}$	C$\Delta^{9\,\sharp11\,13}$	C, E, G, B, D, F$\sharp$, A
Minor		
Cmin	C–, Cm	C, E$\flat$, G
Cmin2	C–2, Cm2	C, D, E$\flat$, G
Cmin6	C–6, Cm6	C, E$\flat$, G, A
Cmin7	C–7, Cm7	C, E$\flat$, G, B$\flat$
Cmin^{maj7}	C–^{maj7}, Cm^{maj7}, C–Δ, CmΔ	C, E$\flat$, G, B
Cmin7$^{\flat5}$	C–7$^{\flat5}$, Cm7$^{\flat5}$, C$\emptyset$	C, E$\flat$, G$\flat$, B$\flat$
Cmin6/9	C–6^9, Cm6^9	C, E$\flat$, G, A, D
Cmin7^9	C–7^9, Cm7^9	C, E$\flat$, G, B$\flat$, D
Cmin$^{maj7\,9}$	C–$^{maj7\,9}$, Cm$^{maj7\,9}$	C, E$\flat$, G, B, D
Cmin7$^{9\,\flat5}$	C–7$^{9\,\flat5}$, Cm7$^{9\,\flat5}$	C, E$\flat$, G$\flat$, B$\flat$, D
Cmin7$^{\flat6}$	C–7$^{\flat6}$, Cm7$^{\flat6}$	C, E$\flat$, G, A$\flat$, B$\flat$
Cmin7$^{9\,\flat6}$	C–7$^{9\,\flat6}$, Cm7$^{9\,\flat6}$	C, E$\flat$, G, A$\flat$, B$\flat$, D
Cmin7$^{\flat9\,11(omit3)}$	C–$^{\flat9\,11(omit3)}$, Cm$^{\flat9\,11(omit3)}$	C, G, B$\flat$, D$\flat$, F, A
Diminished		
Cdim	C°	C, E$\flat$, G$\flat$, A
Cdim7	C°7	C, E$\flat$, G$\flat$, A, B

Steps (1 = R)	Full name
1, 3, 5	C major
1, 4, 5	C suspended (four)
1, 2, 3, 5	C two
1, 2, 5	C suspended (two)
1, 3, 5, 6	C six
1, 3, 5, 7	C major seven
1, 3, 5, 6, 9	C six nine
1, 3, 5, 7, 9	C major seven nine
1, 3, ♭5	C half-diminished
1, 3, ♯5	C augmented
1, 3, ♯4, 5	C sharp four
1, 3, ♯5, 7	C major seven sharp five
1, 3, ♭5, 7	C major seven flat five
1, 3, 5, 7, ♯11	C major seven sharp eleven
1, 3, 5, 7, 9, ♯11	C major seven nine sharp eleven
1, 3, 5, ♭6, 7	C major seven flat six
1, 3, 5, ♭6, 7, 9	C major seven nine flat six
1, 3, 5, 7, 9, 13	C major seven nine thirteen
1, 3, 5, 7, 9, ♯11, 13	C major seven nine sharp eleven thirteen
1, ♭3, 5	C minor
1, 2, ♭3, 5	C minor two
1, ♭3, 5, 6	C minor six
1, ♭3, 5, ♭7	C minor seven
1, ♭3, 5, 7	C minor/major seven
1, ♭3, ♭5, ♭7	C half-diminished
1, ♭3, 5, 6, 9	C minor six nine
1, ♭3, 5, ♭7, 9	C minor seven nine
1, ♭3, 5, 7, 9	C minor/major seven nine
1, ♭3, ♭5, ♭7, 9	C minor seven flat five
1, ♭3, 5, ♭6, ♭7	C minor seven flat six
1, ♭3, 5, ♭6, ♭7, 9	C minor seven nine flat six
1, 5, ♭7, ♭9, 11	C minor seven flat nine eleven omit three
1, ♭3, ♭5, 6	C diminished
1, ♭3, ♭5, 6, 7	C diminished seven

181

Chord symbol	Alternative symbols	Pitches (C)
Dominant		
C7	–	C, E, G, B♭
C7sus4	C11	C, F, G, B♭
C7$^{♭5}$	–	C, E, G♭, B♭
C7^{9}	C9	C, E, G, B♭, D
C7$^{9\ sus4}$	–	C, F, G, B♭, D
C7$^{9\,♯5}$	–	C, E, G♯, B♭, D
C7$^{9\,♭6}$	–	C, E, G, A♭, B♭, D
C7$^{9\,♯11}$	–	C, E, G, B♭, D, F♯
C7$^{♭9}$	–	C, E, G, B♭, D♭
C7$^{♭5\,♭9}$	–	C, E, G♭, B♭, D♭
C7$^{♭9\,♯11}$	–	C, E, G, B♭, D♭, F♯
C7$^{♯9}$	–	C, E, G, B♭, D♯
C7$^{♯9\,♯11}$	–	C, E, G, B♭, D♯, F♯
C7$^{♭5\,♯9}$	C7alt	C, E, G♯, B♭, D♯
C7$^{♭5\,♯9\,♯11}$	C7alt	C, E, G♯, B♭, D♯, F♯
C7$^{9\ 13}$	–	C, E, G, B♭, D, A
C7$^{9\,♯11\ 13}$	–	C, E, G, B♭, D, F♯, A
C7$^{♭9\ 13}$	–	C, E, G, B♭, D♭, A
C7$^{♭9\,♯11\ 13}$	–	C, E, G, B♭, D♭, F♯, A
C7$^{♯9\,♯11\ 13}$	–	C, E, G, B♭, D♯, F♯, A
C7$^{♯9\,♯11\,♭13}$	C7alt	C, E, G, B♭, D♯, F♯, A♭
C7$^{sus4\ 9\ 13}$	–	C, E, F, B♭, D, A
C7$^{sus4\,♭9\ 13}$	–	C, E, F, B♭, D♭, A

Continued from page 179.

- An added 7 indicates that a minor seven should be added: The chord C7 (a dominant or dominant 7 chord) consists of the notes C–E–G–B♭ (R–3–5–♭7). Together, the 3 and the ♭7 make this chord sound a bit bluesy.

- If maj7 is added to the root note (e.g., Cmaj7), the fourth pitch is a major seven. C major 7 consists of the pitches C–E–G–B (R–3–5–7).

- The 6 in a major 6 chord adds a major six to the chord. For example, C6 is C–E–G–A (R–3–5–6).

- A 9 in a C chord adds a high D to the chord.

- A ♭9 adds a lowered nine (D); a ♯9 adds a raised nine (D♯).

Steps (1 = R)	Full name
1, 3, 5, ♭7	C seven / C dominant seven
1, 4, 5, ♭7	C seven suspended four
1, 3, ♭5, ♭7	C seven flat five
1, 3, 5, ♭7, 9	C seven nine
1, 4, 5, ♭7, 9	C seven nine suspended four
1, 3, ♯5, ♭7, 9	C seven nine sharp five
1, 3, 5, ♭6, ♭7, 9	C seven nine flat six
1, 3, 5, ♭7, 9, ♯11	C seven nine sharp eleven
1, 3, 5, b7, b9	C seven flat nine
1, 3, ♭5, ♭7, ♭9	C seven flat five flat nine
1, 3, 5, ♭7, ♭9, ♯11	C seven flat nine sharp eleven
1, 3, 5, ♭7, ♯9	C seven sharp nine
1, 3, 5, ♭7, ♯9, ♯11	C seven sharp nine sharp eleven
1, 3, ♯5, ♭7, ♯9	C seven sharp five sharp nine
1, 3, ♯5, ♭7, ♯9, ♯11	C seven sharp five sharp nine sharp eleven
1, 3, 5, ♭7, 9, 13	C seven nine thirteen
1, 3, 5, ♭7, 9, ♯11, 13	C seven nine sharp eleven thirteen
1, 3, 5, ♭7, ♭9, 13	C seven flat nine thirteen
1, 3, 5, ♭7, ♭9, ♯11, 13	C seven flat nine sharp eleven thirteen
1, 3, 5, ♭7, ♯9, ♯11, 13	C seven sharp nine sharp eleven thirteen
1, 3, 5, ♭7, ♯9, ♯11, ♭13	C seven sharp nine sharp eleven flat thirteen
1, 3, 4, ♭7, 9, 13	C seven suspended four nine thirteen
1, 3, 4, ♭7, ♭9, 13	C seven suspended four flat nine thirteen

• You can also add an 11 or a 13, for example.

The same pitch
In other countries, ♯9 may be indicated as ♭10. These notes sound exactly the same pitch (in a C chord, they're D♯ and E♭). In a chord, these notes have the same function, as they sound the same pitch, just like a raised four sounds the same pitch (F♯, in the key of C) as a lowered five (G♭).

No 13 and ♭13
The chords on pages 190–213 show the main chords with extensions up to and including ♯11. Extensions such as 13 and ♭13 are not included. *Tip:* In chord symbols, ♭13 is sometimes written as ♯5.

TIP

Double sharp, double flat

In some chords, raised or lowered notes need to be raised or lowered once more. For example, turning F♯ major (F♯–A♯ –C♯) into an F♯ augmented chord raises the C♯ once more. Officially, this turns it into a C double-sharp. In daily use — and in this book — this tone is typically indicated by the name of the pitch that it sounds, the D. Likewise, a raised B is called a C, rather than a B sharp (B♯). Note that you will find some double-sharps and double-flats in the chords on pages 190–213.

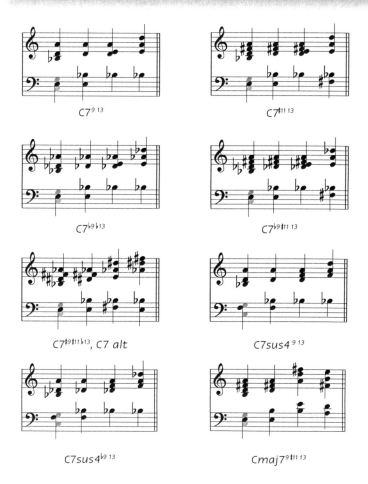

$C7^{9\ 13}$

$C7^{♯11\ 13}$

$C7^{♭9\ ♭13}$

$C7^{♭9\ ♯11\ 13}$

$C7^{♯9♯11♭13}$, C7 alt

$C7sus4^{9\ 13}$

$C7sus4^{♭9\ 13}$

$Cmaj7^{9\ ♯11\ 13}$

If so, you may be looking at an altered chord: a chord in which all pitches except 1 and 3 have been altered. On the opposite page are some examples of chords with an added 13. The information on the previous pages allows you to construct these chords for other root notes too. Some 13 and ♭13 chords are also included in the table on pages 180–183.

Not required

Extensions add color and character to a chord — but you're not required to play all of them at all times. If you're accompanying a soloist, for example, it's typically sufficient to play the R, 3, 5, and 7 of a given chord. So if the chord symbol reads C7$^{♭9♯11}$, for example, you can simply play C7.

Leave out other pitches

You can also choose to leave out other pitches, as long as you realize that the character or timbre of a chord is mainly determined by its 3 and 7. If you play in a band, you can usually leave out the root note; the bass player will play this note. The 5 can often be omitted too. On pages 190–213, the notes that can be left out are marked grey (for chords made up of five or more pitches only).

Add pitches

You may also want to add pitches to a chord. For example, a 9 can be great addition to a maj7 chord (R–3–5–7–9).

Two hands

Chords that are made up of four or more pitches are easier to play if you use both hands — and you can do so too for chords with three pitches, of course. Using both hands allows you to spread the notes over the keyboard (*open voicings*) rather than playing them close together (*closed voicings*). More tips:

- If you use both hands, it may be tempting to **double certain notes** — but you shouldn't, except maybe for the 7. Doubling the 7 helps to enhance the chord.

- Experiment with **closed and open voicings**. For example, play the 1 (C) of Cmaj7 with your left hand, and play 3, 5 and 7 to the right.

185

• If you're playing **with a band**, the bassist playing the root notes, you can play the 3 with your left hand and use your right hand for the 5 and the 7. You may consider adding a 9 to the chord, as suggested earlier; play it between the 3 and the 5, in this particular case.

Omit

Sometimes, the composer or arranger tells you which pitches to leave out, adding the word 'omit' to the chord symbol. The illustration at the bottom of this page shows you an example. The opposite also happens, using the word 'add' to indicate an extra extension. For example, you normally would not play the 3 in a C7$^{\text{sus4}}$ chord, but it can sound really nice. If the composer wants you to add that 3, the chord symbol will read C7$^{\text{sus4(add3)}}$. Actually, this 3 is a bit misleading as you're supposed to play it as an additional higher note, the 10: both the 3 and the 10 are an E, in this chord. Played with two hands, this chord looks like this:

C7sus4$^{(add3)}$
played with
two hands

Extensions and alternatives

You can opt for a closed voicing by replacing chord extensions. For example, you may play a ♯4 rather than a ♯11 (in a C chord, both are F♯s), or replace a ♭9 by a ♭2. As you may have noted, it's simply a matter of subtracting 7 (11-7=4, 9-7=2, etc.). Still, you're usually

C−7$^{♭9\ 11(omit\ 3)}$

Played as the chord symbol
suggests.

C−7$^{♭9\ 11(omit\ 3)}$

Replacing ♭9 (D♭) by a ♭2 and
the 11 (F) by a 4 (right).

supposed to play the extensions at their original pitches, i.e., higher than the other notes of the chord — but some chords tend to sound better if you don't. The opposite page shows an example of such a chord: C–7$^{\flat 9\ 11}$(omit 3), played as suggested by the chord symbol, and using replacement notes for the $\flat 9$ and the 11.

INVERSIONS

Basically, you can play the pitches of a chord in any order you like. If the root note is the lowest pitch of the chord, you're playing the chord in its root position (R–3–5).

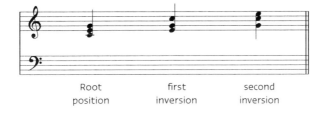

| Root position | first inversion | second inversion |

- If you make the 3 the lowest pitch, you're playing the **first inversion**: 3–5–R.

- The **second inversion** starts with the 5 as the lowest pitch: 5–R–3.

Easier
Inversions can make it a lot easier to go from one chord to the other. For example, you need to really 'jump' when you go from C major to G major in their root positions. Now play C major in its second inversion (G–C–E), and go to G major in its root position (G–B–D): all you have to do is move two fingers. Apart from being easier, this sounds better too. As a general rule: If the next chord has one or two notes in common with the previous chord, play them on the same keys. The less you move, the easier it will be and the better you will sound.

187

Inversions and octaves

Pages 190–213 show the root position and various inversions for every chord (some including the root note as an — additional — lowest pitch). There are many more ways to play all of these chords, so feel free to experiment. One obvious variation is to simply play the chords in a different octave. For example, the second inversion of the C major chord can be played starting on G4 (the G above Middle C), or an octave lower, G3 being the lowest pitch. Tip: Smaller intervals may produce a droning, blurred sound when played below C3.

More pitches

Additional pitches allow for additional inversions, of course. In a major7 chord, for example, the root position would be R–3–5–7, followed by the first inversion (3–5–7–R), the second (5–7–R–3), and the third inversion (7–R–3–5), as shown below.

Cmaj7: root position and first, second, and third inversions.

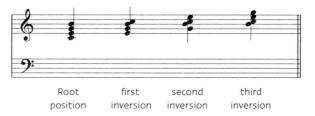

| Root position | first inversion | second inversion | third inversion |

Example

Here's another example of how inverting chords can help you sound better and make playing easier. If you look at the two chords below, you will see that they have the notes G and B in

C major played as G–C–E (left) and G–C–E (right)

G–C–E   G–C–E

common, so you should invert the chords in a way that allows you to keep your fingers on those two keys.

Two ways to go from G7 to C major 7. Inverting both chords makes things a lot easier.

C

Three-note chords

Major

C

Csus4

Major with ♭5 / ♯5

C♭5

Minor

Cmin

Diminished

Cdim

Four-note chords

Major

Csus2, C2   C6   Cmaj7

Major chords with accidentals

C♯4   Cmaj7♯5   Cmaj7♭5

Minor

Cmin2   Cmin6   Cmin7

Minor chords with accidentals

Caug   Cmin^maj7   Cmin7♭5

Dominant

C7   C7sus4

Dominant chords with accidentals

C7♭5

Diminished

Cdim

Five-note chords

Major

Dominant

Major chords with accidentals

Dominant chords with accidentals

Minor

Minor chords with accidentals

Diminished

C6/9   Cmaj7⁹   C7⁹   C7⁹ ˢᵘˢ⁴

Cmaj7♯11   Cmaj9♯11   C7⁹♯5   C7⁹♭6

Cmaj7♭6   Cmaj9♭6   C7⁹♯11   C7♭9

Cmin6⁹   Cmin7⁹   C7♭5♭9   C7♭9♯11

Cmin^maj7 9   Cmin7♭5   C7♯9   C7♯9♯11

Cmin7♭6   Cmin7♭5♭6   C7♯5♯9, C7alt   C7♯5♯9♯11, C7alt

C–7♭9 11(omit. 3)   Cdim7

Enharmonic: C#

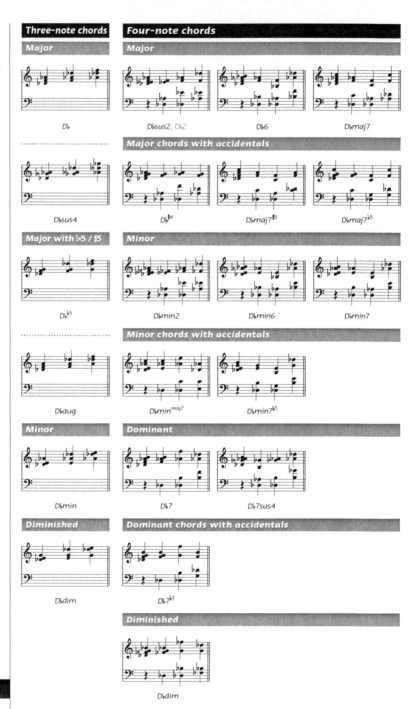

Three-note chords

Major

Db

Dbsus4

Major with b5 / #5

Db b5

Dbaug

Minor

Dbmin

Diminished

Dbdim

Four-note chords

Major

Dbsus2; Db2   Db6   Dbmaj7

Major chords with accidentals

Db #4   Dbmaj7#5   Dbmaj7b5

Minor

Dbmin2   Dbmin6   Dbmin7

Minor chords with accidentals

Dbmin maj7   Dbmin7b5

Dominant

Db7   Db7sus4

Dominant chords with accidentals

Db7b5

Diminished

Dbdim

192

Five-note chords

Db

Enharmonic: C#

Major

Db6/9

Dbmaj7⁹

Major chords with accidentals

Dbmaj7#11

Dbmaj9#11

Dbmaj7♭6

Dbmaj9♭6

Minor

Dbmin6⁹

Dbmin7⁹

Minor chords with accidentals

Dbmin^maj7 9

Dbmin7♭5

Dbmin7♭6

Dbmin7♭6 9

Db-7♭9 11(omit 3)

Dominant

Db7⁹

Db7⁹ sus4

Dominant chords with accidentals

Db7⁹#5

Db7⁹♭6

Db7⁹#11

Db7♭9

Db7♭5♭9

Db7♭9#11

Db7#9

Db7#9#11

Db7#5#9, Db7alt

Db7#5#9#11, Db7alt

Diminished

Dbdim7

D

Five-note chords

D

Major

D6/9   Dmaj7⁹

Major chords with accidentals

Dmaj7♯11   Dmaj9♯11

Dmaj7♭6   Dmaj9♭6

Minor

Dmin6⁹   Dmin7⁹

Minor chords with accidentals

Dmin^maj7 9   Dmin7♭9♭5

Dmin7♭6   Dmin7♭9♭6

D−7♭9 11(omit 3)

Dominant

D7⁹   D7⁹ sus4

Dominant chords with accidentals

D7⁹♯5   D7⁹♭6

D7⁹♯11   D7♭9

D7♭5♭9   D7♭9♯11

D7♯9   D7♯9♯11

D7♯5♯9, D7alt   D7♯5♯9♯11, D7alt

Diminished

Ddim7

Enharmonic: D♯

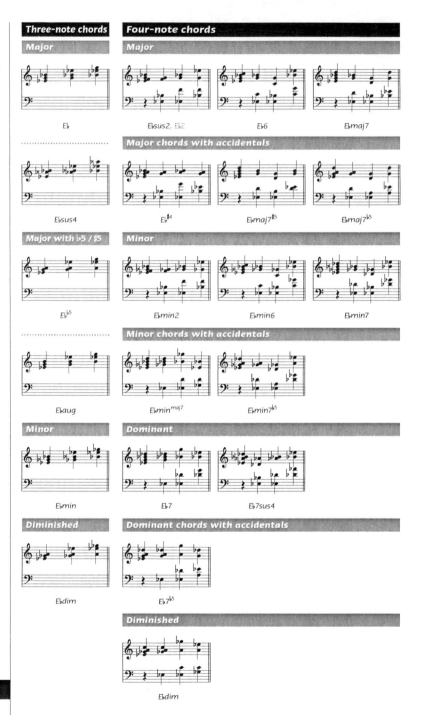

E♭

Enharmonic: D♯

Five-note chords

Major

E♭6/9

E♭maj7⁹

Major chords with accidentals

E♭maj7♯11

E♭maj9♯11

E♭maj7♭6

E♭maj9♭6

Minor

E♭min6⁹

E♭min7⁹

Minor chords with accidentals

E♭min^maj7 9

E♭min7⁹♭5

E♭min7♭6

E♭min7⁹♭6

E♭−7♭9 11(omit 3)

Dominant

E♭7⁹

E♭7⁹ sus4

Dominant chords with accidentals

E♭7⁰♯5

E♭7⁹♭6

E♭7⁹♯11

E♭7♭9

E♭7♭5♭9

E♭7♭9♯11

E♭7♯9

E♭7♯9♯11

E♭7♯5♯9, E♭7alt

E♭7♯5♯9♯11, E♭7alt

Diminished

E♭dim7

E

Three-note chords	Four-note chords

Major / **Major**

E — Esus2, E2 — E6 — Emaj7

Major chords with accidentals

Esus4 — E♯4 — Emaj7♯5 — Emaj7♭5

Major with ♭5 / ♯5 / **Minor**

E♭5 — Emin2 — Emin6 — Emin7

Minor chords with accidentals

Eaug — Emin^maj7 — Emin7♭5

Minor / **Dominant**

Emin — E7 — E7sus4

Diminished / **Dominant chords with accidentals**

Edim — E7♭5

Diminished

Edim

E

Five-note chords

Major

E6/9   Emaj7⁹

Major chords with accidentals

Emaj7♯11   Emaj9♯11

Emaj7♭6   Emaj9♭6

Minor

Emin6⁹   Emin7⁹

Minor chords with accidentals

Emin^maj7 9   Emin7⁹♭5

Emin7♭6   Emin7⁹♭6

E-7♭9 11(omit 3)

Dominant

E7⁹   E7⁹ sus4

Dominant chords with accidentals

E7⁹♯5   E7⁹♭6

E7⁹♯11   E7♭9

E7♭5♭9   E7♭9♯11

E7♯9   E7♭9♯11

E7♯5♯9, E7alt   E7♯5♭9♯11, E7alt

Diminished

Edim7

199

F

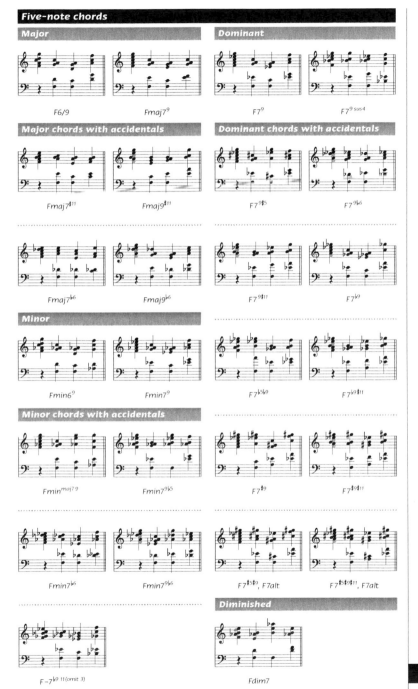

G♭

Enharmonic: F#

Three-note chords

Major

G♭

G♭sus4

Major with ♭5 / #5

G♭♭5

G♭aug

Minor

G♭min

Diminished

G♭dim

Four-note chords

Major

G♭sus2, G♭2   G♭6   G♭maj7

Major chords with accidentals

G♭#4   G♭maj7#5   G♭maj7♭5

Minor

G♭min2   G♭min6   G♭min7

Minor chords with accidentals

G♭min^maj7   G♭min7♭5

Dominant

G♭7   G♭7sus4

Dominant chords with accidentals

G♭7♭5

Diminished

G♭dim

Five-note chords

Major

G♭6/9   G♭maj7⁹

Major chords with accidentals

G♭maj7♯11   G♭maj9♯11

G♭maj7♭6   G♭maj9♭6

Minor

G♭min6⁹   G♭min7⁹

Minor chords with accidentals

G♭min^maj7 9   G♭min7⁹♭5

G♭min7♭6   G♭min7⁹♭6

G♭−7♭9 11(omit 3)

Dominant

G♭7⁹   G♭7⁹ sus4

Dominant chords with accidentals

G♭7⁹♯5   G♭7⁹♭6

G♭7⁹♯11   G♭7♭9

G♭7♭5♭9   G♭7♭9♯11

G♭7♯9   G♭7♯9♯11

G♭7♯5♯9, G♭7alt   G♭7♯5♯9♯11, G♭7alt

Diminished

G♭dim7

203

G

Three-note chords

Major

G

Gsus4

Major with ♭5 / ♯5

G♭5

Gaug

Minor

Gmin

Diminished

Gdim

Four-note chords

Major

Gsus2, G2

G6

Gmaj7

Major chords with accidentals

G♯4

Gmaj7♯5

Gmaj7♭5

Minor

Gmin2

Gmin6

Gmin7

Minor chords with accidentals

Gmin^maj7

Gmin7♭5

Dominant

G7

G7sus4

Dominant chords with accidentals

G7♭5

Diminished

Cdim

G

Five-note chords

Major

G6/9

Gmaj7⁹

Major chords with accidentals

Gmaj7$^{\sharp 11}$

Gmaj9$^{\sharp 11}$

Gmaj7$^{\flat 6}$

Gmaj9$^{\flat 6}$

Minor

Gmin6⁹

Gmin7⁹

Minor chords with accidentals

Gmin$^{maj7\,9}$

Gmin7$^{9\flat 5}$

Gmin7$^{\flat 6}$

Gmin7$^{9\flat 6}$

G−7$^{\flat 9\,11(omit\,3)}$

Dominant

G7⁹

G7$^{9\,sus4}$

Dominant chords with accidentals

G7$^{9\sharp 5}$

G7$^{9\flat 6}$

G7$^{9\sharp 11}$

G7$^{\flat 9}$

G7$^{\flat 5\flat 9}$

G7$^{\flat 9\sharp 11}$

G7$^{\sharp 9}$

G7$^{\sharp 9\sharp 11}$

G7$^{\sharp 5\sharp 9}$, G7alt

G7$^{\sharp 5\sharp 9\sharp 11}$, G7alt

Diminished

Gdim7

205

A♭

Enharmonic: G♯

Enharmonic: G#

Five-note chords

Major

Ab6/9

Abmaj7⁹

Major chords with accidentals

Abmaj7#11

Abmaj9#11

Abmaj7♭6

Abmaj9♭6

Minor

Abmin6⁹

Abmin7⁹

Minor chords with accidentals

Abmin^maj7 9

Abmin7⁹♭5

Abmin7♭6

Abmin7⁹♭6

Ab−7♭9 11(omit 3)

Dominant

Ab7⁹

Ab7⁹ sus4

Dominant chords with accidentals

Ab7⁹#5

Ab7⁹♭6

Ab7⁹#11

Ab7♭9

Ab7♭5♭9

Ab7♭9#11

Ab7#9

Ab7#9#11

Ab7#5#9, Ab7alt

Ab7#5#9#11, Ab7alt

Diminished

Abdim7

207

A

Three-note chords	Four-note chords

Major | **Major**

A — Asus2, A2 — A6 — Amaj7

Major chords with accidentals

Asus4 — A#4 — Amaj7#5 — Amaj7b5

Major with b5 / #5 | **Minor**

Ab5 — Amin2 — Amin6 — Amin7

Minor chords with accidentals

Aaug — Aminmaj7 — Amin7b5

Minor | **Dominant**

Amin — A7 — A7sus4

Diminished | **Dominant chords with accidentals**

Adim — A7b5

Diminished

Adim

Five-note chords

Major

A6/9 Amaj7⁹

Dominant

A7⁹ A7⁹ ˢᵘˢ⁴

Major chords with accidentals

Amaj7♯11 Amaj9♯11

Dominant chords with accidentals

A7⁹♯5 A7⁹♭6

Amaj7♭6 Amaj9♭6

A7⁹♯11 A7♭9

Minor

Amin6⁹ Amin7⁹

A7♭5♭9 A7♭9♯11

Minor chords with accidentals

Amin^maj7 9 Amin7⁹♭5

A7♯9 A7♯9♯11

Amin7♭6 Amin7⁹♭6

A7♯5♯9, A7alt A7♯5♯9♯11, A7alt

Diminished

A–7♭9 11(omit 3) Adim7

209

TIPBOOK PIANO

B♭

Enharmonic: A♯

Five-note chords

Major

Bb6/9

Bbmaj7^9

Major chords with accidentals

Bbmaj7$^{\sharp 11}$

Bbmaj9$^{\sharp 11}$

Bbmaj7$^{\flat 6}$

Bbmaj9$^{\flat 6}$

Minor

Bbmin6^9

Bbmin7^9

Minor chords with accidentals

Bbmin$^{maj7\,9}$

Bbmin7$^{9\flat 5}$

Bbmin7$^{\flat 6}$

Bbmin7$^{9\flat 6}$

Bb–7$^{\flat 9\,11(omit\,3)}$

Dominant

Bb7^9

Bb7$^{9\,sus4}$

Dominant chords with accidentals

Bb7$^{9\sharp 5}$

Bb7$^{9\flat 6}$

Bb7$^{9\sharp 11}$

Bb7$^{\flat 9}$

Bb7$^{\flat 5\flat 9}$

Bb7$^{\flat 9\sharp 11}$

Bb7$^{\sharp 9}$

Bb7$^{\sharp 9\sharp 11}$

Bb7$^{\sharp 5\sharp 9}$, Bb7alt

Bb7$^{\sharp 5\sharp 9\sharp 11}$, Bb7alt

Diminished

Bbdim7

Bb

Enharmonic: A♯

B

Three-note chords	Four-note chords		
Major	**Major**		

B · Bsus2, B2 · B6 · Bmaj7

Major chords with accidentals

Bsus4 · B♯4 · Bmaj7♯5 · Bmaj7♭5

Minor with ♭5 / ♯5 · **Minor**

B♭5 · Bmin6 · Bmin6 · Bmin7

Minor chords with accidentals

Baug · Bmin^maj7 · Bmin7♭5

Minor · **Dominant**

Bmin · B7 · B7sus4

Diminished · **Dominant chords with accidentals**

Bdim · B7♭5

Diminished

Bdim7

Five-note chords

B♭

Enharmonic: A♯

Major

B♭6/9   B♭maj7⁹

Major chords with accidentals

B♭maj7♯11   B♭maj9♯11

B♭maj7♭6   B♭maj9♭6

Minor

B♭min6⁹   B♭min7⁹

Minor chords with accidentals

B♭min^maj7 9   B♭min7♭5♭9

B♭min7♭6   B♭min7♭9♭6

B♭-7♭9 11(omit 3)

Dominant

B♭7⁹   B♭7⁹ sus4

Dominant chords with accidentals

B♭7⁹♯5   B♭7⁹♭6

B♭7⁹♯11   B♭7♭9

B♭7♭5♭9   B♭7♭9♯11

B♭7♯9   B♭7♭9♯11

B♭7♯5♯9, B♭7alt   B♭7♯5♯9♯11, B♭7alt

Diminished

B♭dim7

B

Five-note chords

Major

B6/9

Bmaj7⁹

Major chords with accidentals

Bmaj7♯11

Bmaj9♯11

Bmaj7♭6

Bmaj9♭6

Minor

Bmin6⁹

Bmin7⁹

Minor chords with accidentals

Bmin^maj7 9

Bmin7♭♭5

Bmin7♭6

Bmin7♭♭6

B−7♭9 11(omit 3)

Dominant

B7⁹

B7⁹ sus4

Dominant chords with accidentals

B7⁹♯5

B7⁹♭6

B7⁹♯11

B7♭9

B7♭5♭9

B7♭9 ♯11

B7♯9

B7♯9♯11

B7♯5♯9, B7alt

B7♯5♯9♯11, B7alt

Diminished

Bdim7

Essential Data

If you want to sell your instrument, if something happens to it or it needs repairing, it's always helpful to have all the relevant data at hand. Here are two pages to make those notes. You can also list when your piano is due for another tuning, and any questions you want to ask your piano technician.

INSURANCE

Company:

Phone: Email:

Agent:

Phone: Email:

Policy no.:   Premium:

INSTRUMENTS AND ACCESSORIES

Make and type:

Serial number: Price:

Color/model:

Date of purchase:

Place of purchase:

Phone: Email:

TUNER/TECHNICIAN

Name:

Address:

Phone: Fax:

Email:

QUESTIONS FOR YOUR TUNER / TECHNICIAN

TUNINGS

Next tuning date	Notes

INDEX

Please check out the glossary on pages 163–167 for additional definitions of the terms used in this book.

217

The Tipbook Series

*Did you like this Tipbook? There are also Tipbooks for your fellow
band or orchestra members! The Tipbook Series features various
books on musical instruments, including the singing voice, in
addition to Tipbook Music on Paper, Tipbook Amplifiers and
Effects, and Tipbook Music for Kids and Teens – a Guide for
Parents.*

*Every Tipbook is a highly accessible and easy-to-read
compilation of the knowledge and expertise of numerous
musicians, teachers, technicians, and other experts,
written for musicians of all ages, at all levels, and in any
style of music. Please check www.tipbook.com for up to
date information on the Tipbook Series!*

*All Tipbooks come with Tipcodes that offer additional
information, sound files and short movies at www.tipbook.com*

Instrument Tipbooks

All instrument Tipbooks offer a wealth of highly accessible, yet well-founded
information on one or more closely related instruments. The first chapters of
each Tipbook explain the very basics of the instrument(s), explaining all the
parts and what they do, describing what's involved in learning to play, and
indicating typical instrument prices. The core chapters, addressing advanced
players as well, turn you into an instant expert on the instrument. This
knowledge allows you to make an informed purchase and get the most out of
your instrument. Comprehensive chapters on maintenance, intonation, and
tuning are also included, as well a brief section on the history, the family, and
the production of the instrument.

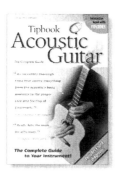

Tipbook Acoustic Guitar – $14.95

Tipbook Acoustic Guitar explains all of the elements
that allow you to recognize and judge a guitar's
timbre, performance, and playability, focusing on
both steel-string and nylon-string instruments.
There are chapters covering the various types of
strings and their characteristics, and there's plenty
of helpful information on changing and cleaning
strings, on tuning and maintenance, and even on the
care of your fingernails.

219

Tipbook Amplifiers and Effects – $14.99

Whether you need a guitar amp, a sound system, a multi-effects unit for a bass guitar, or a keyboard amplifier, *Tipbook Amplifiers and Effects* helps you to make a good choice. Two chapters explain general features (controls, equalizers, speakers, MIDI, etc.) and figures (watts, ohms, impedance, etc.), and further chapters cover the specifics of guitar amps, bass amps, keyboard amps, acoustic amps, and sound systems. Effects and effect units are dealt with in detail, and there are also chapters on microphones and pickups, and cables and wireless systems.

Tipbook Cello – $14.95

Cellists can find everything they need to know about their instrument in *Tipbook Cello*. The book gives you tips on how to select an instrument and choose a bow, tells you all about the various types of strings and rosins, and gives you helpful tips on the maintenance and tuning of your instrument. Basic information on electric cellos is included as well!

Tipbook Clarinet – $14.99

Tipbook Clarinet sheds light on every element of this fascinating instrument. The knowledge presented in this guide makes trying out and selecting a clarinet much easier, and it turns you into an instant expert on offset and in-line trill keys, rounded or French-style keys, and all other aspects of the instrument. Special chapters are devoted to reeds (selecting, testing, and adjusting reeds), mouthpieces and ligatures, and maintenance.

Tipbook Electric Guitar and Bass Guitar – $14.95

Electric guitars and bass guitars come in many shapes and sizes. *Tipbook Electric Guitar and Bass Guitar* explains all of their features and characteristics, from neck profiles, frets, and types of wood to different types of pickups, tuning machines, and — of course — strings. Tuning and advanced do-it-yourself intonation techniques are included.

Tipbook Drums – $14.95

A drum is a drum is a drum? Not true — and *Tipbook Drums* tells you all the ins and outs of their differences, from the type of wood to the dimensions of the shell, the shape of the bearing edge, and the drum's hardware. Special chapters discuss selecting drum sticks, drum heads, and cymbals. Tuning and muffling, two techniques a drummer must master to make the instrument sound as good as it can, are covered in detail, providing step-by-step instructions.

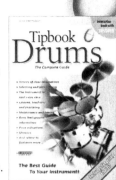

Tipbook Flute and Piccolo – $14.99

Flute prices range from a few hundred to fifty thousand dollars and more. *Tipbook Flute and Piccolo* tells you how workmanship, materials, and other elements make for different instruments with vastly different prices, and teaches you how to find the instrument that best suits your or your child's needs. Open-hole or closed-hole keys, a B-foot or a C-foot, split-E or donut, inline or offset G? You'll be able to answer all these questions — and more — after reading this guide.

Tipbook Keyboard and Digital Piano – $14.99

Buying a home keyboard or a digital piano may find you confronted with numerous unfamiliar terms. *Tipbook Keyboard and Digital Piano* explains all of them in a very easy-to-read fashion — from hammer action and non-weighted keys to MIDI, layers and splits, arpeggiators and sequencers, expression pedals and multi-switches, and more, including special chapters on how to judge the instrument's sound, accompaniment systems, and the various types of connections these instruments offer.

Tipbook Music for Kids and Teens – a Guide for Parents – $14.99

How do you inspire children to play music? How do you inspire them to practice? What can you do to help them select an instrument, to reduce stage fright, or to practice effectively? What can you do to make practice fun? How do you reduce sound levels and

221

prevent hearing damage? These and many more questions are dealt with in *Tipbook Music for Kids and Teens – a Guide for Parents and Caregivers*. The book addresses all subjects related to the musical education of children from pre-birth to pre-adulthood.

Tipbook Music on Paper – $14.99

Tipbook Music on Paper – Basic Theory offers everything you need to read and understand the language of music. The book presumes no prior understanding of theory and begins with the basics, explaining standard notation, but moves on to advanced topics such as odd time signatures and transposing music in a fashion that makes things really easy to understand.

Tipbook Piano – $14.99

Choosing a piano becomes a lot easier with the knowledge provided in *Tipbook Piano*, which makes for a better understanding of this complex, expensive instrument without going into too much detail. How to judge and compare piano keyboards and pedals, the influence of the instrument's dimensions, different types of cabinets, how to judge an instrument's timbre, the difference between laminated and solid wood soundboards, accessories, hybrid and digital pianos, and why tuning and regulation are so important: Everything is covered in this handy guide.

Tipbook Saxophone – $14.95

At first glance, all alto saxophones look alike. And all tenor saxophones do too — yet they all play and sound different from each other. *Tipbook Saxophone* discusses the instrument in detail, explaining the key system and the use of additional keys, the different types of pads, corks, and springs, mouthpieces and how they influence timbre and playability, reeds (and how to select and adjust them) and much more. Fingering charts are also included!